A guide to the

Book of Heaven

Luisa Piccarreta's writings
evaluated in the light
of Catholic doctrine

Stephen Patton

Nihil obstat:
Rev. James Narithookil, C.M.I., Censor Librorum Deputatus

Imprimatur:
Most. Rev. Jaime Soto, Bishop of Sacramento
October 9, 2013

Cover photo and layout by Mother Julie Stephens, MMJC

To Walter Berg
(1919-2011)

Walter was my father-in-law and
the greatest man I have ever known.

Acknowledgements

I once heard that behind any man who has accomplished anything there stands a woman… rolling her eyes. In the case of this book, that woman of course is my wife, Bridget. Even if she never actually rolled her eyes behind me, she nevertheless not only patiently endured the many hours that this book has taken – hours that kept me away from her and the demands of our family life – but she also continuously supported, encouraged and prayed for me. Next after my baptism, she is my life's greatest blessing.

Mother Ellen Mary Berg, MMJC, first introduced Bridget and me to the writings of Luisa Piccarreta almost twenty years ago. Ever since then she has never ceased to encourage and pray for me that I might better understand – and help others better understand – Luisa's spirituality. She is indeed the patroness of this book.

When I asked Mother Julie Stephens, MMJC, if she would help with the layout and design of this book she was quick and happy to agree. The cover photo that she took of the trees at the Trappist Abbey in Vina, California reflects the order, peace and beauty of her own soul. The considerable time and talent that she devoted to this project are deeply appreciated.

Table of Contents

Introduction

Books with eye-popping titles are notorious for failing to deliver, but the one given to Luisa Piccarreta's spiritual diary – *Book of Heaven: the Recall of the Creature to the Order, the Place and the Purpose for which It was created by God* – was so extraordinary that I had to take a look.

Toward the end of the nineteen century and continuing through much of the first half of the twentieth, Jesus had appeared and spoken to this poor, simple and devout woman in southern Italy. Her account of these interactions with him would eventually fill 36 volumes and two associated books of prayer. The early years were as profound as one might expect from such an interaction, but otherwise were not remarkably different from the accounts of scores of saints and mystics. Eventually, though, Jesus would make it clear that he had singled her out in an unprecedented way. My fascination grew, but eventually so did my concerns.

It was one thing for Jesus to invite Luisa to embrace the spiritual practices of "living in the divine will" which, he explained, was not only the original spiritual state of Adam and Eve but also the summit of spiritual perfection. But it was quite another to claim that no other person since the Blessed Virgin Mary, including the holiest of saints in the history of the Church, had ever attained it. He told Luisa that she was to be the first since Mary to live once again in that exalted spiritual state. Others would come after her, that is, as they would learn and apply what he was teaching her.

Then, as if that claim were not ambitious and disconcerting enough, Jesus told Luisa that his revelation to her, and her response to it (followed by the responses of others), constituted the "third fiat of God", which would somehow complete his first fiat of Creation and his second fiat of Redemption. In other words, her private revelation would in some way consummate God's original and ultimate purposes for man and the universe.

Could such stunning claims be reconciled with Scripture and Catholic teaching? Was her revelation really divine in origin after all? It turns out that others had similar concerns.

Soon after I started reading Luisa's writings I discovered that a handful of American writers had begun to circulate negative opinions of them. As drawn as I was to her writings, in a certain sense I welcomed this development. I wanted to see some in-depth analysis, but at that time, 1997, the only secondary literature I could find were either biographies about Luisa or summaries of her spirituality. I was not aware of any critical theological commentary of any kind – new or old, negative or positive. So I thought that even if I disagreed with what these writers had written I would at least have something substantial to engage with. I did bring a predisposition to their opinions, though.

While I was open to being convinced by these writers, I also believed that Luisa's writings, like anyone's, deserved the benefit of any and all reasonable doubt. To borrow from the widely-recognized legal principle, the burden of proof should rest upon the prosecution, and mere suspicions or lingering uncertainties about guilt are not enough to convict. Luisa's writings, in short, were entitled to be considered orthodox until they were clearly and convincingly proven to be heterodox.

Applying this standard, I found that these writers had not met their burden of proof. While on some issues I might have agreed with their underlying sentiments of concern and discomfort, still I knew this was not sufficient to establish their claims. Even if some of Luisa's themes might on the surface seem inflated, odd, unfamiliar or even delusional, so long as they reasonably *could* be viewed within a basic framework of orthodoxy, then that is how they would be *entitled* to be viewed.

Still, even though I was not convinced by these writers, I believed that what they had written could serve to begin a dialogue that would eventually help everyone – including me – reach a better understanding of the issues. If what Luisa had written was indeed of God and intended by him for wide circulation, then it was critical that it be understood properly.

So in 1999 I wrote a treatise, *The Orthodoxy of Luisa Piccarreta's Writings: A Response to Certain Doctrinal Objections*. In two ways I demonstrated the insufficiency of the arguments that had been posited: 1) by showing how their characterizations of Luisa's passages and themes were either unbalanced, taken out of context or otherwise non-representative, and 2) by showing how each of Luisa's challenged passages and themes could be reasonably and fairly viewed within the boundaries of Catholic doctrine. I concluded that until and unless her writings could be clearly and convincingly shown to be heterodox, they were entitled to be considered orthodox. (Hence the title I chose.)

I first privately mailed copies to the two principle objectors, asking for their replies. When neither wrote back, I offered the paper for posting on a public website (www.transporter.com) that contained the original objections of these two writers along with other related documents. I hoped these writers would eventually thoughtfully respond, but neither they nor anyone else ever did.

While this silence gave me some assurance that what I had written was on the right track, I did not consider that 1999 treatise to be an end-product. The most that could be said for it is that it had successfully rebutted some objections raised by some people. A need remained for a more comprehensive theological study guide, one that would supply a framework of orthodoxy that would both allay the concerns of anyone troubled by Luisa's writings, and also provide clear doctrinal guidance to those drawn to them.

Over these fourteen years since then I have continued developing my thoughts about these matters and, as time has allowed, also privately writing about them. The occasion that has now prompted me to offer this study guide is Archbishop Giovanni Battista Pichierri's "Communication No. 3" of November 1, 2012. Addressed to anyone and everyone interested in Luisa and her spirituality, Archbishop Pichierri reiterates a concern he had expressed in his 2006 letter:

4

I still observe with sorrow that "the doctrine of the Divine Will has not always been presented in a correct and respectful way, according to the doctrine and Magisterium of the Church, putting remarks in the mouth of Luisa that are not even implicitly found in her writings. This provokes a trauma in consciences and even confusion and rejection among the people and by some Priests and Bishops" (*Letter* of March 9, 2006).

It is especially sad that Archbishop Pichierri's concerns, reiterated six and half years later, are apparently directed not to those opposed to or bothered by Luisa's doctrine of the Divine Will, but to those supportive of it. It would seem that the zeal of even well-meaning devotees, when it is unbridled from Catholic doctrine, can turn destructive and divisive. But how many of these people have been doing this innocently and unwittingly? How can they stay surely within the limits of Catholic doctrine without a reliable guide outlining those limits? He went on to express another concern.

He had recently received a communication regarding Luisa's cause from the Vatican's Congregation for the Causes of Saints advising him that "before proceeding *any further*, an examination of the writings of the Servant of God will be done, in order to clarify difficulties of a theological nature." (Emphasis in the original.) We are left to speculate about what theological difficulties the Holy See had identified, but what matters is that they had found some difficulties with the writings themselves, and not just in the sometimes misguided interpretations of those reading and circulating them.

Archbishop Pichierri qualifies this comment from the Vatican by emphasizing that no competent ecclesiastical authority, which would include the Holy See, himself and his predecessors, has ever pronounced that Luisa's writings contain any doctrinal errors. In other words, "difficulties of a theological nature" are not the equivalent of "doctrinal errors." Indeed there have been many occasions over the long, unfolding history of the Church when it has not been entirely clear whether a new theological proposition or spiritual theme from a private revelation corresponds with Catholic doctrine. On many of these occasions the Church has undertaken a careful and thoughtful examination of the person's writings. That is precisely what the Holy See is now doing with Luisa's writings.[1]

What are we to do in the meantime? Archbishop Pichierri writes, "In the anticipation of the judgment by competent Authority, I invite you to make more serious and in-depth meditations and reflections in your personal reading on these writings in light of Sacred Scripture, Tradition and the Magisterium of the Church."

And so I offer this study guide in response to Archbishop Pichierri's invitation, that is, to assist the faithful in a more serious and in-depth reading of Luisa's literature in light of Catholic doctrine.

---

[1] It should also be noted that this examination is being conducted in a positive context. It is not that the Holy See is scrutinizing Luisa's writings as if they were the suspect writings of a questionable Catholic theologian. They are being examined only because she is being considered for elevation to the altar of the Church's Saints and Blesseds.

Goal and outline

My goal in this study is modest. I do not offer a full account of either Luisa's life or her spiritual doctrine. Many others have done this quite well both in books and in talks. My goal is to summarize, analyze and evaluate Luisa's dominant spiritual themes in light of Catholic doctrine, and correspondingly offer those themes a comprehensive framework of orthodoxy. I wish to demonstrate for those who might be troubled by her doctrine that it *can* be reconciled with Catholic teaching while simultaneously showing those enamored of her doctrine that it *must* be reconciled with Catholic teaching.

I do not re-visit every objection that I addressed in my 1999 study, especially the ones of lesser substance such as claims of Monothelistism and Quietism. If readers are concerned about those issues they should review that earlier study. I have limited my focus here upon the weightiest theological issues, indeed the ones I suspect will be of greatest interest and concern to the Holy See.

I have written this guide hoping it to be both substantial enough for priests, religious, theologians and anyone else schooled in theology while still being clear and simple enough to be understandable and user-friendly to those without theological training. I admit that as between these two readerships I have inclined my style more toward the former than the latter. But this should not be taken to mean that Luisa's spirituality itself is best left to the academics and the intellectuals. On the contrary, Jesus wanted it for everyone, regardless of their education. Luisa herself, who had only limited education, is the preeminent example.

7

Rather, I offer my thoughts in a more academic form only because of the weight and the complexity of the underlying doctrinal issues.

But indeed for the sake of all, regardless of their education, and most especially for those who wish not only to study Luisa's writings but also to apply them in their lives, I have added reflection questions at the end of each of the main sections of this study guide. I wrote these with both Luisa's writings and Catholic doctrine in mind, hoping to guide the reader to a richer, more fully Catholic embrace of the doctrine of the Divine Will.

This study is divided into three main evaluative sections, followed by a section of conclusions and recommendations. Here is a summary of each.

1. *Luisa's Obedience: the Key to her Life, Writings and Spirituality.* To adequately evaluate and emulate the spiritual themes found in Luisa's writings requires appreciating the context in which she wrote. This means most especially appreciating that she wrote in a posture of radical obedience. Her obedience surely demonstrates her humility, which is an authenticator of any mystical experience. But in her case it also carries an even greater significance. It was not only that she as a Christian soul obediently and wholly submitted her will to the authority of the Church. She also obediently and wholly submitted the very substance of what she wrote to that same authority. That is, both she and the ministers appointed to care for her understood that their role was not only to test her content for error, but also to expound upon it, as needs be, to ensure that it would be understood only within the boundaries and aims of divine Revelation. In her

mind then, the Church bore an indispensable role in the authentic interpretation and transmission of her revelations from Jesus. We can consequently conclude that the interpretive authority the Church presently possesses with respect to her writings is absolute.

2. *Living in the Divine Will.* The central theme of Luisa's writings is that God created the human will not only to obey the divine will in everything but also to "co-operate" with it. Man enjoyed this state in his original innocence, lost it through the fall, but had it reclaimed for him by Christ. Jesus describes this state of "living in the divine will" as a state of mystical union in which man – with, through and in Christ – becomes so completely absorbed in God that he shares in God's own eternal act. As is typical of mystical literature, the terms Luisa employs to describe this absorption can be at times obscure and seemingly exaggerated. It is clear, however, that she did not intend to promote a literal obliteration of the human will. Rather, she promoted a co-ordination of wills that essentially corresponds to, even if it would appear to exponentially exceed, the forms of mystical union to which the saints have testified over the centuries.

3. *The Third Fiat of God.* Luisa reported Jesus characterizing living in the divine will as not only the highest possible state of mystical union that man can attain in this life, but as a state never before attained by anyone in the Church other than the Virgin Mary and Christ himself. Moreover, he characterizes the effecting of this new spiritual state in man as the Third Fiat and claims that it will complete the work he set in motion in the First Fiat of Creation and in the Second Fiat of the Redemption. He avoids characterizing this divine initiative as a new dispensation of grace and similarly avoids

characterizing his revelation to Luisa as completing or surpassing his one, definitive self-Revelation. Rather, he characterizes this divine initiative as a dramatic, unexpected actualization of graces already and always contained within the new order of the redemption. He similarly characterizes his revelation to her as a profound explication of his definitive self-Revelation that will bring its ultimate aims to consummation.

4. *Conclusions and Recommendations.* So long as Luisa's writings are read as she intended them to be read, they not only correspond with Catholic teaching but they bear the potential of dramatically advancing the ultimate purposes of the Church, namely, the consummate sanctification of man and the concomitant glorification of God in creation. However, in their original form her writings do not offer a self-evident interpretive framework adequate to ensure that interpretations – especially those regarding the third fiat of God – stay within the boundaries of Catholic doctrine. Knowing this, she not only accepted the fact that her writings would be published with some form of an official Church commentary, she welcomed it.

The authority of this study

Is this study guide just such an "official Church commentary"? No, it is not. I point this out in light of a concern Archbishop Pichierri had first raised in 2007 and then reiterated in his November 1, 2012 letter:

> "From the moment that the Diocesan Inquiry was begun, the Archdiocese has never officially

designated any Theologian or Censor for the writing of Luisa…" (*Communication* of April 23, 2007).

Why would the Archbishop insist – twice – that no theologian is, or ever has been, designated to speak for the Archdiocese or for Luisa's cause? Because one or more persons have been presuming to do exactly that. And so I wish to make it clear that by offering this study guide I do not presume to speak for anyone other than myself.

What I offer here I offer only in my private capacity as a Catholic. Its only weight of authority is the strength of its analyses. While the reader can be assured by this study guide's *nihil obstat* and *imprimatur* that it does not contain matter contrary to Catholic faith and morals, still, these official marks should not be understood as an official adoption or endorsement by the Church of Luisa's writings. Indeed, regarding the official status of Luisa's writings – and the relationship of this book to them – I should make another clarification.

As of this writing, the Church has not yet published a comprehensive, final and official (formally known as a "typical and critical") edition of Luisa's writings. What has been made available of her writings – both in print and through the internet (and sometimes in contradiction to the instructions of the Archdiocese) – is not yet in the final form that it needs and deserves to be in, and which – as I will demonstrate in the first section – Jesus intended it to be in. So, in a certain sense, I am offering this book as a guide to writings that are not yet published.

But I offer it nevertheless for two reasons. First, at this time there is no official guide supplied by the Church. I expect that when the Archdiocese publishes the definitive edition it will contain not only the edited, full body of Luisa's writings, but also all the guidance necessary to properly understand them. But that has not yet been provided.

Second, the fact is that such theological and pastoral guidance is currently and clearly needed. Even though the writings are not in their final form and even though their ongoing publication is not officially sanctioned, they continue to proliferate throughout the world. Not surprisingly, along with this proliferation has come misinterpretation and confusion.

And so until the Church publishes the final and official edition of Luisa's writings and, along with it, the guidance that is needed, I offer this guide as a stopgap. The reader should understand, though, that whenever and however the Church does publish a definitive commentary, which, in whatever form it would take, would come *only* from either the Archdiocese or from the Holy See, then everything I offer in this guide should be interpreted – and indeed rejected if necessary – in light of it.

It was clear that Luisa wished everything that she wrote to be understood in conformity with Catholic doctrine and in continuity with the Church's great spiritual tradition. I offer this work with the hope of helping the reader do just that.

Stephen Patton, M.A., J.D.
Sacramento, California
December 2013

I.

LUISA'S OBEDIENCE: THE KEY
TO HER LIFE, WRITINGS AND SPIRITUALITY

Modern advances in historical – critical methodology have made it clear that unless adequate consideration is given to the context in which a piece of literature was written, the writer's meaning often cannot be fully appreciated. The Fathers of the Second Vatican Council recognized that this principle is crucial for the proper interpretation of Scripture:

> Hence the exegete must look for that meaning which the sacred writer, in a determined situation and given the circumstances of his time and culture, intended to express and did in fact express, through the medium of a contemporary literary form. Rightly to understand what the sacred author wanted to affirm in his work, due attention must be paid both to the customary and characteristic patterns of perception, speech and narrative which prevailed at the age of the sacred writer, and the conventions which the people of his time followed in their dealings with one another.[2]

If understanding the "determined situation" of a writer is, as a general principle, important in understanding his meaning, in the case of Luisa Piccarreta it is vitally so. It is not that her literature, seen in isolation from the circumstances under which she wrote, is without substantial

---

[2] *Dei Verbum*, 12.

meaning. Rather, one aspect of those circumstances forms an interpretive key that is indispensable to unlocking the deepest and clearest sense of her meaning. That aspect is the history and nature of her obedience to the ministers of the Church.

Luisa was a diminutive, minimally educated and otherwise unremarkable daughter of a poor, farm working family in the southeastern Italian city of Corato. She lived from 1865 to 1947. From an early age she was intensely devoted to Jesus, and in her teen years she began to experience mystical encounters with him, encounters that would endure for most of her life. Her 36 volume diary, which spanned some forty years, and two books of meditation – one on the passion of Our Lord and the other on the interior life of Our Lady – represent the written account of these private revelations.

From a close reading of Luisa's writings and the secondary literature – including letters to and from her and biographies and testimonials about her – I have not sensed the least shadow of fraud. On the contrary, all the evidence points to her integrity as a person and as a writer. The account of her conversations with Jesus satisfies all the criteria of authenticity that one would normally look for in a visionary: emotional stability, self-doubt, fear of delusion, revulsion for notoriety, desire for hiddenness, firmness in virtue, continuous participation in the sacraments, and a meticulous and constant submission and obedience to ecclesiastical authority.[3] It is apparent, though, that among these criteria

---

[3] Arguably missing is the desire that the revelations cease. But it is clear from her diary entries that Luisa's only desire was for the solace she

the last was not only evident in Luisa's life, but evident to an extraordinary degree. I will first review the facts and then discuss the impact I think they have on the Church's present effort to evaluate her meaning.

As a teenager Luisa had accepted, at Jesus' invitation, the life of a victim soul. Soon after, she was suffering profoundly – physically, emotionally and spiritually – and her sphere of activity became correspondingly more limited. Eventually, her sufferings confined her to bed, where she would remain for the rest of her life. She began to fall periodically into states of semi-paralysis, unable to move her arms or her mouth. Ultimately, these episodes of paralysis became total and death-like.

She could be removed from one of these episodes only by the prayer of a priest spoken in her presence. Unfortunately many of the priests of the area who knew of her condition considered her a nuisance, and most were reluctant to come to her aid. Consequently Luisa sometimes remained in this agonizing state for days on end. When a priest finally would come to release her, he would often go on to scold her for making a pest of herself. Her diary testifies that she suffered acutely from the misunderstandings and doubts of these priests and that she prayed that they should not have to come to revive her. Jesus, however, not only refused to grant her request but seems to have intended that entire sphere of her mystical sufferings to remain continuously subject to the authority of priests – even though most of them at the

---

received from Jesus, not for the extraordinary phenomenon of the revelation itself.

15

beginning of her sufferings did not consider them to be authentic.

Eventually the Archbishop at that time, Mons. Giuseppe B. Dottula, came to know about what was happening with her, and in 1886 he delegated Fr. Michele De Benedictis to be her special confessor. This priest recognized the authenticity of her sufferings and came to see her daily. She began to disclose her interior life to him. As soon as he learned that she had offered herself to Jesus as victim, he ordered her not to accept any more sufferings without his permission. Her diary, supported by the testimony of all who knew her, shows that Luisa understood this, and every direction of Fr. Benedictis – and the directions of each priest after him who cared for her – to be a voice of authority over and above the voice that she heard in her intimate conversations with Jesus.

Indeed she recorded that Jesus himself repeatedly insisted upon her fidelity to holy obedience, and there are episodes in which he would test her resolve. Jesus would come to her and invite her to share in his sufferings, and though she dearly wanted to do so, she would refuse, because Fr. Benedictis had so instructed her. It was not until Fr. Benedictis finally gave Luisa probationary permission to resume the state of a victim soul that she would again accept Jesus' invitations.

All the available evidence then indicates that from the very beginning of Luisa's extraordinary experience as a victim soul she was aware that God intended it to be subject to the rightful authority of the Church in the most radical way.

That same disposition would extend to her experience as a writer as well.

Early in 1899 the new prelate, Archbishop Tommaso de Stefano, appointed a new confessor for Luisa: Fr. Gennaro de Gennaro. Almost immediately he commanded Luisa to begin writing down all that took place (and all that had taken place) between her and Jesus. From the opening line of the spiritual diary she then began to write until she was finally given permission to cease writing some forty years later, it is clear that she wrote only in obedience to Fr. Gennaro and to his successors. She would have preferred her life, and especially her interior life, to remain perpetually hidden. Entries like, "I would do anything not to have to refer to myself on paper," are found throughout the 36 volumes she eventually filled.

Luisa's life-long submission and obedience to ecclesiastical authority was, on the one hand, only what one would expect from someone in her situation. Obedience is, after all, a fruit and a hallmark of any authentic spiritual experience. But on the other hand, the particular context within which she received and recorded her private revelation seems to indicate that her submission and obedience had an even greater significance.

She apparently wrote with the understanding that the role of the priests in authority over her was not simply to check her private revelation against Church teaching as in a pass-fail litmus test. She understood that they, and the Catholic doctrine they represented, were indispensable to the proper interpretation and transmission of its content. Indeed she seems to have viewed their role as, in some way, intrinsic to the revelation itself.

The Role of Saint Annibale Di Francia

Luisa's relationship with Saint Annibale Di Francia provides the most abundant insights into her relationship with the ministers of the Church, and the corresponding relationship of her private revelation to Church teaching. Long before meeting Luisa, Fr. Annibale had been renowned for fidelity to Church teaching and discernment of private revelations. Three years before his first meeting with Luisa in 1910, in a letter to Abbot Combe, Saint Annibale had written:

> What God works in private in the Church must be submitted to the judgment of those who represent Him. God is jealous of this order he established and wants no one to alter this rule of faith. When people deal with high personalities of the holy Church to make them accept private revelations or works, they must act with great humility and submission to the Church's authority. They must act humbly and prudently to gain their assent and the approbation of the ecclesiastical authorities.[4]

Would he consider Luisa as an exception to these standards? In his General Preface to her writings, he does, in fact, put her in a unique category:

---

[4]*The Father's Letters*, translated from the Italian by Fr. Rosario Scazzi, RCJ, edited by Mary Western and Fr. John Bruno, RCJ, Ad Usum Privatum Pro Manuscripto (General Curia of the Rogationist Fathers, Rome, 1992), p. 113.

It seems that Our Lord, who century after century increases the wonders of His Love more and more, wanted to make of this virgin with no education, whom He calls the littlest one that He found on earth, the instrument of a mission so sublime that no other can be compared to it - that is, the triumph of the Divine Will upon the whole earth, in conformity with what is said in the "Our Father": Fiat Voluntas Tua sicut in Coelo et in terra.[5]

And yet, despite his opinion of her exalted mission, Saint Annibale did not consider her revelation to be exempt either from the rule of perpetual submission to Church teaching and ecclesiastical authority or from the possibility of error in the form of its transmission. He explained this in a letter to her:

> ...pray most humbly and with great fervor... because we do not have any room for error in something this delicate; ...may a divine light assist the writer and interpreters and compiler, so that nothing might be added to, nor taken from, the boundaries of divine revelation, which must conform to divine prudence regarding everything that must be accommodated and dealt with in the presence of such great supernatural Revelations that pass through a human channel, a channel that is not always totally immune

---

[5] Messina, October 29, 1926.

from subjective imperfections which are not culpable but accidental, just like the mystics teach.[6]

St. Annibale understands that for the transmission of this revelation to be proper and adequate "a divine light" had to be at work not only in Luisa, the writer, but in the "interpreters and compiler" as well. Why? To make sure that it stays within "the boundaries of divine revelation." He thus views Luisa's revelation as a profound message from God intended for all mankind, but nevertheless not yet in its final form.

There is no indication that Luisa would have been surprised by, or that she would have resisted, Saint Annibale's suggestion of an official editing of her writings. Indeed all the evidence is to the contrary. Long before meeting him she had anticipated the need for just such gifts of discernment as he and others in authority over her could give. Just months after beginning her diary, in her entry of January 8, 1900, she had written: "Who knows how many blunders, how many errors these things that I write contain?" She recounts Jesus' response:

> My daughter, even the errors will help to make known that there is no deceit on your part and that you are not some doctor (for if you were, you yourself would have known where you erred). These will also make it more clear that it is I who speak to you – when the thing is seen simply. But I assure you that

[6] Di Francia, Saint Annibale, *Collection of Letters sent by Blessed Hannibal Di Francia to the Servant of God, Luisa Piccarreta*, (Jacksonville, 1997), pp. 16 - 17.

they will find no shadow of vice, nor anything that does not say 'Virtue'; for, as you write, I Myself am guiding your hand. At the most, they shall be able to find something which, at first glance, seems erroneous. But if they will look at it very closely, they shall find the Truth.

Luisa seems to be aware that some of her expressions could give the impression of doctrinal error. But she does not know exactly which ones. She understands that Jesus agrees – yes, there are apparent errors – but rather than pointing them out to her and showing her how to correct them, he allows them for a reason. There will be a subsequent scrutiny of some kind, and Luisa is likely comforted to know that through it the Truth shall be found despite her errors of expression.

Toward the end of his life, as his health began to fail, Saint Annibale reiterated his concerns. Despite the confidence he had maintained in her writings, he wished nevertheless to revise some of her expressions:

> I should read over your original Volumes, because, believe me, in several places, it is necessary to make some changes in order to obtain the correct meaning of the word. I was doing this revision with great love, chapter by chapter, but since I became sick I could not do anything any more. Nevertheless it is a necessary job. There are some points which, inasmuch as they are true and holy if seen in the right spirit and with holy simplicity, still are not fit for publication. They

would be criticized by the Ecclesiastical Authorities, and this fact might jeopardize the whole Work.[7]

He does not specify the problems he had seen or what changes and revisions he thought would be necessary "to obtain the correct meaning" from Luisa's original volumes. But clearly he believed that until that could be done, her writings, at least in part, were "not fit for publication." His concern about drawing criticism from the Ecclesiastical Authorities was – it would seem – a premonition of what would in fact occur eleven years after his death.

Luisa's corresponding attitude is in clear agreement:

> You tell me that certain chapters of my manuscript should not be printed and certainly it should not be done, because I have written only to obey. I would like that you not even let them be copied, marking them with a sign of the cross, or with 2 hyphens, signaling to those who do the copies to pass over where those marks are found, since what should interest you is to make known the Will of God and the great good that comes to us by doing it. All the rest, and especially that which pertains to me, you should put aside.[8]

---

[7] Di Francia, Letters to Luisa, *ibid*, p. 38.
[8] Letter from Luisa to Father Annibale, 29 March 1925, Archives of the Rogationist Postulation (Rome), [Archivio Postulazione Rogazionisti – Roma] Inventory No. 5854.

In another letter to Luisa, Saint Annibale wrote about copying the second volume of her diary. He told her that he had instructed the copy-writer to leave space…

> …in the margin (so) I can make the necessary corrections, because sometimes your explanations are not clear, besides the very many spelling errors and many pages with faded ink. At times I must add some defining notes according to the lights which the Lord deigns to grant me.[9]

Luisa's corresponding agreement about the need for divinely guided, supplementary corrections and explanations is again clear:

> I read the Chapter which you sent me from Volume 17, and I am surprised in seeing how Our Lord has given you so much light in clarifying it so well. Oh, yes! The angels will assist you to assure that everything remains clarified, in order that the Divine Volition be known and loved.[10]

> I do not hide from you the fact that to carry out exactly the obedience as your Paternity tells me to, I would have to keep you nearby, in order to assure me of the truth, and then I would be able to write faithfully everything, everything. Because many things, after the light of the presence of Sweet Jesus

---

[9] Di Francia, Letters to Luisa, *Ibid*, p. 25.
[10] Letter from Luisa to Father Annibale, 11 February 1926, Archives of the Rogationist Postulation (Rome), [Archivio Postulazione Rogazionisti – Roma] Inventory No. 5868.

has passed, I cannot see clearly and for fear of making an error, I pass over writing them down. But, however, in my soul, I try to take in as much as I can and to put into practice the light of truth which Jesus has brought me.[11]

In regards to the fact that in the writings many things are not expressed well, you are right. But all the bad (error) is because we are distant from each other. Because of those things that are not well expressed, (you will find) the rest of this light that is missing in me. Therefore, if you are nearby I would tell you immediately about the light that is missing, and then you would have to work less; but also in this, Fiat.[12]

Luisa's and Saint Annibale's shared understanding of his role as her editor was confirmed by Jesus. Though she often recounts Jesus telling her how exalted is the knowledge he reveals to her, indeed, how her writings would be as a "new sun"[13] for the Church, he also confirms the need for official, collateral clarification. In her diary entry of August 18, 1926, (19), Luisa recounts Jesus giving her this message for St. Annibale:

---

[11] Letter from Luisa to Father Annibale, 22 October 1926, Archives of the Rogationist Postulation (Rome), [Archivio Postulazione Rogazionisti – Roma] Inventory No. 5875.

[12] Letter from Luisa to Father Annibale, 27 February 1927, Archives of the Rogationist Postulation (Rome), [Archivio Postulazione Rogazionisti – Roma] Inventory No. 6117.

[13] February 10, 1924, (Volume 16). Hereinafter volume numbers are provided in parenthesis.

My son, the task that I have given you is great; and, therefore, it is necessary that I give you much light to make you understand clearly what I have revealed, because, to the degree to which they are expounded with clarity, to that degree they shall produce their effects.

By this time, the Archbishop of Trani had already given Saint Annibale the task of editing and publishing Luisa's writings, and so it is likely – given her history of obedience – that she would have already been disposed to submit without question to whatever editing he might have suggested. Therefore, this revelation would first of all only confirm how she already viewed that relationship. But it seems to tell us even more about her disposition toward Saint Annibale.

She would have known not only that her volumes in their original form needed to be "expounded with clarity" by someone with ecclesial authority, but also that they would produce little of the effect God intended without that collateral assistance.

In fact, in light of these two overriding concerns – the one Saint Annibale had expressed to Luisa about keeping her writings within the "boundaries of divine revelation" and her own concern about "blunders" and "errors" in her writing – she likely would have thought that without such collateral expounding, her writings could produce an *unintended* effect. That is, to the extent that others would expound her writings in unclear or erroneous ways, most especially by not thoroughly reconciling them to Church teaching, their effect would not only be less than what Jesus had intended, but perhaps even the opposite.

It would seem that that very possibility eventually materialized.

The 1938 Condemnation in Context

Fr. Benedetto Calvi assumed St. Annibale's role as Luisa's editor after his death in 1927. While Fr. Calvi evidently shared his predecessor's enthusiasm for Luisa's writings, he does not appear to have shared the same acute awareness or concern that Saint Annibale had about the doctrinal correctness of some of her themes and forms of expression. For instance, Saint Annibale had published four editions of a work Luisa had written entitled the "Hours of the Passion of Our Lord Jesus Christ with thoughtful reflections and revisions." In his own fifth edition (1934) of this work, Fr. Calvi explains in the preface the rationale for this new edition which the Holy Office[14] would condemn four years later:

> ...my intent in this whole affair was to correct it in its literary form and to render it more in conformity with the original, to reorder it in various parts, to expand it with new writings directly from the original author...I have by no means the intention of either correcting or minimizing what was written by Fr. Annibale. To the contrary I fully and integrally reprinted all that which was in Annibale's version with some necessary variations.[15]

---

[14] The Holy Office was the name at the time for the Vatican's Congregation for the Doctrine of the Faith

[15] Taken from Positio Super Virtutibus, Vol II, Servi Dei Hannibalis Mariae Di Francia, Congregatio Pro Causis Sanctorum, Tipografia Guerra s.r.l., Piazza di Porta Maggiore, 2 (Roma), 1988, p. 715.

To evaluate the changes Fr. Calvi introduced in the 5th edition would require a study beyond the scope of this book. However, the evidence would seem to indicate that despite Fr. Calvi's best intentions he may have effectively undone St. Annibale's previous, successful efforts to conform Luisa's work to Catholic teaching. I say this because in 1988 the Congregation for the Causes of Saints pointed out that the Holy Office's 1938 condemnation of this book should be understood as directed only to Fr. Calvi's fifth edition, and not to the previous four that Saint Annibale had edited.[16] So, ironically, the condemnation of the fifth edition was apparently due – at least in part – to Fr. Calvi's zeal "to render it more in conformity with the original."[17]

The condemnation, it should be noted, does not necessarily constitute a condemnation of the content, which is distinguishable from the form in which it is expressed. The aim of the condemnation is after all to safeguard the faithful who are not always capable of seeing beyond the form to the substantive content. Apart from the weight and merits of the condemnation, though, what matters is that in the minds of both Luisa and her editors, it was they and not she who bore the ultimate responsibility of ensuring that what she wrote was in conformity with Catholic teaching. She did not hand

---

[16] *Ibid.*

[17] To be fair to Fr. Calvi it should be noted that even if Luisa would have absolutely deferred to his judgment and authority on theological matters, still everything he did he did only with her agreement and with the consent of the superior at the time. Moreover, at the time he published the fifth edition the climate of the Church in general, and the Vatican in particular, was contrary to mystical revelations. In such a climate an elevated degree of suspicion and scrutiny would likely have been directed toward the fifth edition.

over her writings to them with instructions not to tamper with them. On the contrary, she trusted that these representatives of Christ and his teachings would edit her writings in whatever manner and to whatever extent they deemed necessary.

Immediately after the condemnation Luisa wrote a profession of obedience and submission to the Magisterium of the Church, and submitted it to her archbishop, asking him to pass it on to the Holy Office. Archbishop Leo, however, told her it was not necessary to send the letter since the confiscation and condemnation had taken place without his or Fr. Calvi's knowledge or consent. The content of that unsent letter, though, tells us much about her willingness to submit her revelation to the authority of the Church:

> With humility, I spontaneously and promptly fulfill my duty as a Christian soul, of offering my unconditional, unhesitating, full and absolute submission to the judgment of the Holy Roman Church. And so, without any restrictions, I disapprove and condemn everything that the Supreme Sacred Congregation of the Holy Office disapproves and condemns in the said books, in the same sense and with the same intention as the Sacred Congregation.

From such a profession of obedience and fidelity I think it fair to conclude that had Luisa been made aware before the condemnation that there were any errors, ambiguities or other difficulties in any of her themes or manners of expression, she would have wanted them either to be

28

conformed to Catholic teaching or not printed at all. She did not trust herself but those who directed her and her confessors.

What Does Luisa's Obedience Mean for Us?

From the very beginning of her mystical experiences Luisa believed that Jesus spoke to her and directed her in two ways: by what he said to her through his private revelations, and by what he said to her through the ministers of his Church and the teaching they represented. Moreover, he made it clear to her – through both mediums – that what he said to her through his ministers was to have an authority over and above what he told her through his private revelation.

It was not that she would have perceived these two mediums in competition with one another. Rather, she would have seen them in a complementary relationship. In other words, Luisa would have known that it was really only one Jesus who was speaking to her, but his one voice was coming to her through a process involving two aspects or forms, one inner and one outer.

The inner form was her private revelation, which she knew she had to obediently submit to the outer form, which was official Church authority and teaching. She knew that what Jesus told her by way of the outer form was to play a crucially important role, namely, to provide a firmly Catholic interpretation and structure to what he told her through the inner form. So, she would have understood Jesus' revelation to her to be a first, raw form that needed Church teaching officially applied to it in order to receive its final form. Only in that way would his words to her, and to the world, achieve their intended effect.

Before attempting to distill some working principles of interpretation and evaluation from Luisa's situation, I should first clarify what should *not* be included among them.

Even if there was a sense in which Luisa expected the ministers of the Church to provide a structure of orthodoxy to her writings, this should not be taken as a license to warp the rules of authentic literary construction. We are not free, for example, simply to delete, alter, or ignore any of her themes or expressions that, by their plain and unavoidable meaning, contradict Catholic teaching. Any changes made to the original text would have to be only to the form of an expression and not to its substance.[18]

The editorial process, in other words, must serve only to assist her revelation along its own true, inner trajectory. It must not replace or redirect that trajectory. Similarly, we must not avoid the question of whether Luisa's spiritual doctrine in fact possesses an orthodox, inner coherence, or whether it can only be made to appear orthodox within a superimposed structure of Catholic teaching that cannot, in fact, be fairly derived from it.

---

[18] To allow for substantive changes would be, in effect, to reduce Luisa's account from a revelation to a meditation. The Congregation for the Doctrine of the Faith pointed out this distinction in its *Notification on Vassula Ryden*: "The fact that the aforementioned errors no longer appear in Ryden's later writings is a sign that the alleged 'heavenly messages' are merely the result of private meditations." As reported in *L'Osservatore Romano*, Weekly Edition in English, 25 October 1995, p. 12.

Finally, in our attempts to view Luisa's revelation within a structure of Catholic teaching we should not, in practical effect, understate, compromise or otherwise depart from her revelation. Though perhaps well intentioned, any such action would not only be dishonest but would also contradict her intent as a writer. On February 24, 1924, (16), Luisa recounts how Jesus explained to her that the Church would never do any such thing to her writings:

> ...the Church has commented on the Gospel and has written much about all that I did and said, but never has it distanced itself from my fountain, from the origin of my teachings. So it will be with my Will. I will put in you the foundation of the Eternal Law of my Will, which is necessary in order to make It, as well as Its teachings, understood. And if the Church explains and clarifies my teaching, she will never depart from Its origin—from the fountain constituted by Me.

Rather, fairness to the situation in which Luisa wrote suggests that the Church should include the following principles in her evaluation of Luisa's writings. Readers should likewise apply these principles in their private reading of her literature:

Luisa's orthodox intent should be presupposed.

There is no evidence that Luisa had any subjective intent to contradict Church teaching. On the contrary, all the evidence indicates that she intended her writings to be understood only in a sense consistent with Catholic teaching. This is not to say that she was plagued with doubt that what she wrote was unclear or erroneous. Indeed this is not what we encounter in her writings. Her ordinary conscience and conviction are that Jesus guides and assists her with clarity and correctness. But she was aware of her human and intellectual limitations. And so, in keeping with her intent, any passages or themes that might be of ambiguous or doubtful meaning should be understood, if it is reasonably possible within the limits of legitimate literary construction, to have that meaning that would conform to Church teaching.

The Church's interpretive authority includes not only evaluating the meaning of Jesus' words to Luisa but also, if necessary, supplying those words with meaning.

Luisa expressed the normal doubts of a person who receives a mystical revelation, but she expressed them within the context of an obedience so radical that it included an unqualified disposition for her writings to be corrected and formed by the ministers of the Church. This is not to say that Luisa or these ministers considered Jesus' meaning to be infinitely malleable. Rather, in those instances in which Jesus' meaning might be ambiguous or otherwise unclear, these representatives of the Church were to enjoy an absolute authority, that is, not only to listen to the text but also to speak to it. Even if the Church might not presently take this authority to the extent of making definitive interpretations about what Jesus' meaning *is*, the Church could, in complete harmony with Luisa's frame of mind, speak with the authority of Jesus and declare what his meaning *is not*. In doing so the Church would be supporting and advancing an objective that is not only her own but also Luisa's, that is, ensuring that the faithful who read Luisa's writings will reach conclusions only within the boundaries of divine Revelation.

The Church's interpretive authority includes making corrections at a grammatical level, clarifications at a semantic level, and explanations at a thematic level.

Luisa's accounts of her communications with Jesus include many spelling and grammatical errors. These errors are not properly attributed to Jesus, because Luisa was not taking direct dictation from him. Rather she was recalling, after the fact and in the best way she could, given her limited education, communications that were essentially interior and mystical in nature. She expected the ministers of the Church to make the necessary corrections. At the semantic level, even though the meaning of her expressions is, on the whole, clear, there are occasions when it is not. In these instances she would have expected the ministers of the Church to clarify the meaning, that is, in light of Catholic teaching. At the more comprehensive, thematic level, Luisa would have likewise expected the ministers of the Church to supply, when necessary, an interpretive framework that would be consistent with Jesus' revelation to her and yet also capable of thoroughly grounding it in Catholic teaching.

Study and Reflection Questions

1. Though Jesus singled out Luisa Piccarreta for a unique and lofty mission, she spurned all attention and public recognition. Do you believe that emulating this trait of Luisa is essential for anyone who wishes

to live in the divine will? Why? Are there any ways in which your human will might be unduly seeking human approval?

2. Luisa wanted only to be small, hidden and alone with Jesus. Who are the small, hidden and alone people in your life, your family, your parish? What can you can learn about true holiness from their example?

3. Luisa lived the evangelical counsel of obedience to a degree unprecedented in the history of the Church. What role do you think obedience to rightful authority should play as you try to live in the divine will? In what areas of your life might you be resisting holy obedience?

4. Imagine three books in front of you: the Bible, the Catholic Catechism, and a volume of Luisa's diary. Discuss the relationship between them. Which has a primacy of authority over which? How should you interpret each in light of the other two?

5. Jesus told St. Annibale, through Luisa, that it was crucial for St. Annibale to expound upon her writings with clarity, ensuring especially that they be understood only within the boundaries of divine revelation. Why would Jesus not have provided this clarity directly to Luisa? Why would St. Annibale's role, and the role of all Church officials after him, be so important in the diffusion of this spirituality?

6. No authentic private revelation is properly understood unless it leads Catholics to a more devout, regular and grateful participation in the sacramental life of the Church. Consider how this was the case with Luisa. How can living in the divine will deepen your appreciation for each of the Sacraments?

II.

LIVING IN THE DIVINE WILL

Overview of Luisa's Spirituality

Most of those who knew Luisa Piccarreta knew her for her life of extraordinary virtue. Few were aware, though, that her inner life was far more extraordinary. It began at an early age.

When she was 9, Luisa began to hear Jesus speaking to her interiorly. First showing her how to overcome her fears, he then began to direct her spiritual life, teaching her how to do all her duties in union with him. More and more she centered her life on the Blessed Sacrament, engendering what would be a life-long devotion. Over time, she developed a habit of continuous conversation with Jesus. Around the age of 13 he directed her to an especially intense effort to mortify her self-will. She later wrote, "Jesus tried to kill my will, even in the smallest things – so that I would live only for Him."[19] At the age of 17 Luisa accepted Jesus' invitation to live as a victim soul.

When she was 22, Fr. Michele de Benedictis gave Luisa permission to return to the state of a victim soul. (For a brief period Fr. Benedictis had instructed her, under obedience, to

---

[19] Date not specified, (1).

withdraw from this state.) From that day until her death almost sixty years later she remained bedridden, living a life of extraordinary penance and reparation. In October of that same year (1888), Jesus gave her the gift of the mystical marriage, a state of mystical union ordinarily understood to be the culmination of the spiritual journey. It would seem, though, that Jesus had more in store for Luisa.

In the months that followed, he prepared her for what he promised would be the consummate state of union between her will and the divine will. This took place in September 1890, when Jesus took her out of her body to Paradise to renew their marriage in the presence of the Trinity. Thereupon he poured a new depth of grace within her. At the time, the full significance of the event escaped Luisa, but years later, after she had begun her spiritual diary, Jesus reminded her of it, and began to gradually explain the distinctive character and importance of this new spiritual state.

With the exception of Our Lady, in all prior experiences of mystical union, the highest God had ever lifted anyone was to a state in which the divine will fully operated in the human will. To Luisa, though, God had given a new privilege. She had become the first person since Our Lady in whom the human will also fully operated in the divine will. This state of "living in the divine will" was, Jesus explained, the highest form of union that is possible in this life between the creature and the Creator.

Adam and Eve had enjoyed this supreme form of union with God in their original innocence, but lost it through the fall. Through the redemption, Jesus completely restored man to his original dignity, and now, through Luisa, he wished to help man more fully realize and reclaim the most profound dimension of that dignity. He summarized his objective in the title he gave Luisa for her spiritual diary: *Book of Heaven: The Recall of the Creature to the Order, the Place and the Purpose for which It was Created by God.*

Distinguishing Characteristics

Luisa's spirituality is not the first to describe the continuum of human perfection in terms of a deepening correspondence of the human will with the divine. It does, however, purport to introduce a new and higher degree to the end of that continuum. The pathway leading to this state remains the same. One still strives to live all the virtues heroically, meet all the duties of his state in life, participate regularly in the sacraments, pray and do penance without ceasing for the salvation of souls, give all credit for his spiritual progress to God and none to self, and commit never to part from the divine will even for an instant. As one faithfully lives this life, he hopes eventually to become so absorbed in union with God that God mystically "takes over" all of his actions. Up to that point, divine will spirituality is virtually indistinguishable from every other form of Christian spirituality.

What Jesus, through Luisa, reveals at the end of this pathway, though, is a vista that opens upon the highest dimension of man's union with God. Jesus wants man to know that God's free gift of the divine indwelling means not only that God has become fully present and active in all of man's temporal actions, but also that man has become fully present and active in all of God's eternal actions. Jesus emphasizes the profoundness of this eternal dimension:

"My daughter, there is a great difference between living united with Me and living in my Will." And while He said that, He pulled me by the arms and said to me: "Come into my Will for even one single instant, and you will see the great difference." I found myself in Jesus. My little atom swam in the Eternal Will. Moreover, since this Eternal Volition is a single Act that contains together all the acts – past, present, and future – I, being in the Eternal Volition, took part in that single Act which contains all acts, inasmuch as it is possible for a creature. I even took part in the acts which do not yet exist, and which must exist, unto the end of centuries, and as long as God will be God... Then, Blessed Jesus said to me: "Have you seen what living in my Will is? It is to disappear. It is to enter into the ambiance of Eternity. It is to penetrate into the Omnipotence of the Eternal, into the Uncreated Mind, and to take part in everything and in each Divine Act inasmuch as it is possible for a creature. It is to enjoy, while remaining on earth, all the Divine qualities."[20]

For man to live in the divine will then, means that he, aware of his nothingness before God, mystically "disappears" on the created, human level, and allows God to be present in all the finite, temporal good that man does. God correspondingly allows man to "re-appear" with him on the uncreated, divine level to be present in all the infinite,

---

[20] April 8, 1918, (12).

eternal good that God does. Jesus explains that Adam enjoyed this state of unity with God before the fall:

> My daughter, in his state of innocence, possessing the life of my Divine Will, Adam possessed the universal life and virtue. Therefore, I found the love of everything and of everyone centralized in his love and in his acts, and all the acts were unified together – not even my works were excluded from his act. I found everything in the works of Adam; I found all the shades of beauties, fullness of love, unreachable and admirable mastery, and then, everything and everyone.[21]

In this original state, Adam enjoyed an extraordinary freedom:

> With the power of Our Divine Fiat he did whatever he wanted; he bilocated in all created things, and if he spoke, if he loved, if he adored and operated, his voice resounded throughout the whole creation, and It was invested by his love, adoration and work. Therefore, the Divinity felt the love, the adoration, the work of His first son in all of His works.[22]

By his disobedience, Adam lost this freedom for himself and for all mankind, but Christ, through his obedience, regained it for man in all of its original fullness:

---

[21] August 12, 1928, (24).
[22] November 10, 1927, (23).

Now, one who lives in my Will rises into the act of innocent Adam, and making the universal life and virtue her own, she makes his act her own. Not only this, but she rises into the acts of the Queen of Heaven, in those of her very Creator, and flowing in all the acts, she centralizes herself in them and says: "Everything is mine, and I give everything to my God... I possess everything and I can give everything, without exhausting anything of my immense riches."[23]

Aware of the new freedom of life in the divine will, Luisa believes her voice and love can reach all times and places:

Continuing to follow the acts of Jesus done in His Divine Will when He was on earth, I was following Mother and Son when they fled to Egypt... How many hidden beauties they possessed; how many varieties of heavens, more beautiful than that which can be seen above our horizon; how many more refulgent suns they contained. And yet, no one could see anything; nothing appeared other than three poor fugitives. Jesus, my Love, I want to follow, step by step, the steps of my Celestial Mama; and as She walks, I want to animate the blades of grass, the atoms of the earth, and make you feel my "I love You" under Her soles. I want to animate all the light of the sun, and, as it shines on your face, I want it to bring You my "I love You"; all the waves of the wind, its caresses – let all say to You: "I love You". I am the one who, in your Fiat, brings You the warmth of the

---

[23] Ibid, August 12, 1928, (24).

sun to warm You, the waves of the wind to caress You, its whistling to speak to You and say: "Dear little One, let everyone know your Divine Will; let It come from within your little Humanity, that It may take Its dominion and form Its Kingdom in the midst of creatures "

Jesus replies:

Oh! How pleasing to Us did your repeated refrains in the wind, in the sun, in the water, under Our steps, reach Us upon the wings of Our Fiat: "I love you, I love you – let your Kingdom come." It was Our echo that we could hear in you, as We wanted nothing but the Divine Will to reign and be the conqueror of all.[24]

Luisa's prayer here illustrates a spiritual practice, central to divine will spirituality, known as praying "the rounds." There are two objects to this prayer: God's work of creation, and his work of redemption.

We begin a "round" of creation recalling that God encloses his love for every person in every created thing, in every moment of its existence. By and through our union with the divine will we are thus each given the capacity to prayerfully, but nonetheless actually, "enter into" any created thing at any moment in time. And so, from within the divine will, we enjoy the freedom to roam with contemplative wonder through time and space, finding (and indeed investing) divine love for all mankind everywhere, giving voice to that love and returning to God a

---

[24] February 9, 1928, (23).

corresponding act of praise, love and thanksgiving. We similarly offer to God each of our daily acts, no matter how insignificant, as an act of praise, love and thanksgiving for his love present throughout creation.

Just as we can share in the eternal dimension of God's loving act of creation, so can we share in the eternal dimension of his loving act of redemption. Praying a "round" of redemption involves entering into the historical events of Christ's passion – principally those events spanning the twenty-four hours from the moment he took leave of his mother to the moment he was taken from the cross – and sharing with him as he suffers and extends his mercy, through those events, to all creatures in all times and places.

And so, to "do" an Hour of the Passion means to read it attentively, meditating on it, contemplating it, making it one's own life. It is not merely compassionately remembering the sufferings of Jesus as events that happened many centuries ago in a far away place. Rather, it is, first of all, to enter into the Divine Will, in which everything is present and *in act*, and to participate in the interior acts and sufferings of Our Lord, which are present and *in act* at this precise moment, so as to repeat His life within us, to grow in His likeness, and to pour upon everyone the infinite value, merits and effects of His Passion.

Jesus explains this difference:

> To repeat my Passion in act in the creature, is different from one who only thinks of my pains and compassionates them. The first is an act of my Life, which takes my place in order to repeat my pains,

44

and I feel I am given back the effects and the value of a Divine Life; while in thinking of my pains and in compassionating Me, it is only the company of the creature that I feel. But do you know in whom I can repeat my pains, in act, of my Passion? In one who has my Will as center of life.[25]

In this spirituality one also prays with special devotion for the fulfillment of the Lord's Prayer petition that the Father's will be done on earth as it is in heaven. Jesus promised Luisa that that petition would indeed be fulfilled as she and others would begin to live in the divine will, that is, following the spiritual practices he describes and corresponding to the graces he offers to make it possible. By once again doing the Father's will as it was done in the beginning, that is, in the heavenly manner of living in it, these children of the divine will would stand before God as the consummation of his recapitulation of man and creation:

> Oh, how the work of Creation will be reflected in them! They will be the triumph of my Redemption - everything shall triumph in them. Then will I be able to say: 'My works are complete', and I will take rest in the midst of the children of my Supreme Fiat.[26]

How living in the divine will is grounded in Christ's Eternal Priesthood.

Living in the divine will is presented in Luisa's diary as a mystical gift that has its origin and perfection in Christ's

---

[25] October 24, 1925 (18).
[26] May 6, 1928, (24).

45

Incarnation and the redemption. By virtue of the hypostatic union the Son of God made each of his human acts not only grace the time and place in which his humanity dwelt, but also reach into God's eternal NOW, that "time and place" which embraces all times and places:

> My daughter, if my Supreme Will had not let my human will enter into the Divine Will, my Humanity, as holy and pure as It is, could not have formed the complete Redemption. My human will would have lacked all-seeingness, and therefore It would not have been able to see everyone. It would have lacked immensity, and would not have been able to embrace all; omnipotence, and would not have been able to save everyone; eternity, and would not have been able to take everything as one single point, and to remedy everything... So, in order to form the Redemption, I did nothing other than open the doors of the Supreme Will to my Humanity – doors which the first man had closed; and giving my Humanity free field, I let It operate the Redemption within the very bosom of the Supreme Will.[27]

Thus, the one historical moment in which Christ, as priest and victim, offered himself up for man, can be said to never end. Diffused into his own divine eternity, his saving work reaches all human generations and forms "the complete redemption." Man is called to respond by uniting himself in every way to Christ's priestly offering, which includes sharing in the eternal dimension of his priesthood. John Paul II describes that response: "The new priestly people which is

---

[27] August 5, 1923, (16).

the Church not only has its authentic image in Christ, but also receives from him a real ontological share in his one eternal priesthood, to which she must conform every aspect of her life."[28]

But exactly how and to what extent does the Church exercise her "real ontological share" in the eternity of Christ's one priesthood? How does she "conform every aspect of her life" to it? Explanations are usually restricted to the ministerial priesthood,[29] and directed toward understanding how these priests, specially configured to Christ, carry on in time his eternal, saving work.[30] But such explanations do not exhaust the central mystery.

Luisa's diary suggests that there is more to man's participation in Christ's eternal priesthood than the manner in which man receives and nurtures the divine indwelling through the sacraments. Namely, that participation also includes the manner in which man, guided by the Spirit, lifts all that he is and does into the humanity of Christ and thus into the eternity of God, and thereby shares in that single, eternal act by which Christ the Eternal Priest creates and redeems the entire created order. Man, as priest, shares in all aspects of God's work of creation and redemption as they

---

[28] *Pastores Dabo Vobis*, 13.

[29] E.g., "Only the Sacrament of Orders gives the ordained minister a particular participation in the office of Christ, the Shepherd and Head, and in his Eternal Priesthood." *Christi Fideles Laici*, 23.

[30] E.g., "(Priests) have been consecrated by God in a new manner at their ordination and made living instruments of Christ the Eternal Priest that they may be able to carry on in time his marvelous work whereby the entire family of man is again made whole by power from above. (Cf. Mal 2:7; 1 Tim 4:11-13; 1 Tim 1:9.)" *Presbyterorum Ordinis*, 12.

are made manifest in all times and places. The gift of living in the divine will then emerges as the consummate mode of a contemplative "co-operation" between God and man, accomplished by and through man's participation in Christ's eternal priestly actions.

This does not mean that living in the divine will reorders either who man is essentially or how he fundamentally relates to God. His identity as a creature remains intact, and he still encounters and responds to his Creator only by the unmerited gift of grace,[31] which is extended to him only in and through Christ's human nature.[32] Rather, that same essential encounter and response is exponentially magnified and extended. To see how that happens we look to the mystery of Christ's own Sacred Humanity.

The Son of God desires, and by his Incarnation he has made it possible, that man share in every dimension, both exterior

---

[31] The fact that living in the divine will is a gift that flows from the gift of sanctifying grace is made clear throughout Luisa's writings, most especially by those passages in which Jesus describes how his mother, the creature par excellence, lived it, e.g., "my Queen Mama possessed the Sun of my Will by grace, and I possessed It by nature." September 8, 1927, (22).

[32] Christ's human nature is entirely unlike the creature's inasmuch as it is filled with a superabundant plenitude of sanctifying grace and is, moreover, the immediate, conjoined instrument of properly divine activity. This means that his human nature living in the divine will is the lone essential means by which any other created nature lives in the divine will (and even exists at all). Any involvement that the creature, in the divine will, might be said to have in the eternal, universal act of creation and redemption is entirely derivative, non-essential and participatory. Everything claimed in Luisa's diary about the value of the creature's acts in the divine will, regardless of how enormous, can nevertheless be understood within the parameters of these principles.

and interior, of the mystery of his own life as a man: "Christ enables us to live in him all that he himself lived, and he lives it in us..."[33] It is by this inestimable gift that any Christian can dare to journey into the deepest core of Jesus' created, human soul, and there unite with him in all that he lived.

However, to Luisa, Jesus yet distinguishes two categories of union with him: a union in which the soul does not consciously and explicitly move, as his human soul did, within the eternity of his divine will, and a union in which the soul does. While souls in either category experience a union with him that is grounded in his humanity, the latter experience it in a greatly expanded sense and manner:

> If the first cooperated with my redemption in order to save souls, to teach the law, to banish sin, being limited within the centuries in which they lived, the second will go beyond, copying what the soul of my Humanity did in the Divine Will. They will embrace all centuries, all creatures, and rising above all, will put in force the rights of Creation which are due to Me, and which concern all creatures, bringing all things to the first origin of Creation and to the purpose for which Creation was delivered. Everything is ordered in Me: if I issued Creation, It must return to Me ordered, just as It came out of my hands.[34]

---

[33] CCC 521.
[34] October 6, 1922, (14).

And so, while living in the divine will should not and need not be seen as a mode of union with God that is new in essence (because it remains grounded in the creature's union with Christ's human nature, made possible only by grace), it can be seen as new in degree, that is, insofar as it opens up from the soul's inner wellspring of sanctifying grace an eternal mode of sharing in God's work.

In one sense everything remains the same for the soul in the divine will, but in another everything changes. For example, in every instance of union with God, it is always the divine indwelling, expressing itself through the foundational, common priesthood of baptism, which prompts all Christian souls "to restore to creation all its original value."[35] In their response, all souls, even the laity, "share in the exercise of the power with which the Risen Christ draws all things to himself and subjects them along with himself to the Father, so that God might be everything to everyone (cf. 1 *Cor* 15:28; *Jn* 12:32)."[36]

However, those souls who purposefully exercise this very same power "in the divine will" can yet hope their restorative prayers and efforts, with and in Christ's, will transcend and bear fruit for the Father even beyond the moment in which they presently dwell. In this way divine will spirituality inspires us not only to restore the fallen world around us, but to enter into Christ's eternal, uncreated divine will (by way of his created human will) and share with him as he restores every shortfall of every creature in every moment of creation's fallen history. Thus, Jesus' call to

---

[35] *Christi Fideles Laici*, 14.
[36] *Ibid.*

the creature in Luisa's diary emerges as a radical magnification and indeed a re-dimensioning of the same call that he has always made to the priesthood of the baptized, that is, to spread the dominion of his kingdom and bring it to its consummation:

> In this kingdom creation itself will be delivered from its slavery to corruption into the freedom of the glory of the sons of God. (Cf Rom. 8, 21) Clearly then a great promise and a great trust is committed to the disciples: "All things are yours, and you are Christ's, and Christ is God's." (I Cor. 3, 23) The faithful, therefore, must learn the deepest meaning and the value of all creation, as well as its role in the harmonious praise of God.[37]

How man, in the divine will, can participate in the divine creative act.

By sharing in Christ's Eternal Priesthood, we share not only in his eternal redemption of the universe, but also in his eternal creation of it. Of course, this needs to be understood properly. The power to create *ex nihilo* belongs only to the divinity. But the Christian tradition has never looked upon the notion of man acting as God's "co-creator" as problematic, that is, so long as it remains clear that man, as creature, receives his existence in every moment only from his Creator, and joins in the creative act only in a participatory sense.

---

[37] *Lumen Gentium*, 36.

And this is indeed the only sense in which Jesus ever expresses the notion to Luisa, albeit in a new and radically expanded dimension:

> And, oh! How my Fiat puts Itself in feast in repeating Its acts – because only in one who lives in It can It have Its act of always creating, things which It has done as well as new things. In fact, the soul lends to It her nothingness emptied, which my Volition uses as the space in order to create what It wants, almost as It used the void of the universe in order to extend the heavens, to create the sun, to put boundaries to the sea, so that the earth might form its beautiful flowerings. And this is the reason why you go around in the acts of my Fiat and as though many waves of light pass through your mind, in which you follow and feel, impressed into yourself, like many scenes, the Creation, man in the act of being created, the Queen of Heaven in the act of being conceived, the Word descending, and many more acts done by my Will: it is the power of my Creating Fiat that wants to always do, always give, without ever ceasing… And do you know how these acts are created in you? As for you, by recalling them, recognizing them and loving them…[38]

Jesus never characterizes the eternal, creative act as proper to man by nature,[39] but chooses verbs such as, "follow," "feel," "recall," "recognize," and "love" to describe man's

---

[38] February 10, 1929, (25).

[39] On the contrary, he makes it clear that, "the right of creating is only of God." March 13, 1927 (21).

participatory involvement. Elsewhere, man is described as "the narrator" who "repeats together with my Will what I did in creating."[40]

It is clear in Luisa's writings that even in the divine will man remains essentially a listening being, capable only of giving what he has first received. In any creative act, he is first, always and only, to be present with God, disposed to receive from him. So long as man remains in that receptive posture, he can receive and echo any act of his Creator:

> My daughter, for one who lives in my Will, there is not one act of Ours at which she is not present, nor any act We released from Ourselves, which she cannot receive.[41]

> My love for one who lives in my divine Will is such that I let her do whatever I do; I give her the right over my acts as if they were hers.[42]

Praying "the rounds of creation" then emerges as a spiritual practice in theological continuity with such traditional prayers as the Canticles of St. Francis and the three Israelite youths (Daniel 3), only with a new and deeper dimension. As the priest of creation, man "gives voice" to divine love present in the beauties of creation and returns to God a hymn of praise and thanksgiving, but he also does so in every moment and corner of created history. Moreover, he

---

[40] May 12, 1929, (26).
[41] April 22, 1927. (21).
[42] July 24, 1938, (36).

shares in the very creative act by which God, in the beginning, invests all of creation with divine love.

How man, in the divine will, can grasp, and participate in, the divine eternity and immensity.

Even if man, in the divine will, can share in God's creative act in this sense, he nevertheless remains limited by his created nature. How is it then that he can grasp and participate in that which is essentially unlimited, that is, his Creator's eternity and immensity?

First, he takes solace in recalling that God never has required him to fully comprehend what it means to participate in any aspect of the divine nature. From the beginning God wished "to share with us divine benefits which entirely surpass the powers of the human mind to understand."[43] That innate limitation of created nature continues with man as God shares with him the gift of living in the divine will.[44] And so the record of Luisa's perceptions of that gift and her understanding of it serves only as a guide to, and not as a gauge of, our reception and utilization of it.[45]

---

[43] *Dei Verbum*, 6.

[44] "My little daughter, ...a continuous act in my Will...is incomprehensible to the created mind." May 4, 1929, (26).

[45] Luisa herself did not always perceive the operations of her will in the divine will. She once lamented, "While I was fusing myself in the holy Divine Volition, I thought to myself: 'Before, when I used to fuse myself in the holy Supreme Volition, Jesus was with me; and together with Him I entered into It; thus, entering was a reality. But now I do not see Him. So I do not know if I enter into the Supreme Volition or not. When I make my beginning act to enter into the Divine Volition, I feel more like someone reciting a memorized lesson, or that these words of entrance are nothing more than a manner of speech.'" Jesus assured her, "My

Second, just as we should not think that we can or need to fully grasp the divine immensity intellectually, neither should we suppose that we can or need to fully possess it ontologically. Our created souls might expand toward the infinite, but they can never contain it. And so, even if it might be said that God, by opening up the gift of the divine will within our souls, can radically expand our capacity to share in his own limitless immensity, never does that capacity itself become limitless:

> My Will fills (the soul who lives in my Will) with such fullness as to leave no empty space within her; and since she is incapable of possessing the whole divine immensity, It fills her for as much as the creature can contain..."[46]

Likewise, it is to Christ's humanity alone that the notion of "infinite merit" can be properly attributed.[47]

In short, this new appreciation of man's integration into the eternity of God need not confuse the attributes of the creature and the Creator. Pius XII could both sympathize with those who "make every effort to understand and to

---

daughter, you must know that whether you see Me or not, each time you fuse yourself in my Will, I, from within your interior, take you by the hand to lift you high; and from Heaven I give you my other hand to take yours and take you in our midst in our interminable Will." January 27, 1925, (17)

[46] October 2, 1927, (23).

[47] This does not, however, preclude Christ from allowing the creature who lives in his divine will to share in his infinite merits, just as his saints in every age have shared in them, but in a new and vastly expanded measure.

clarify the mystery of this our wonderful union with Christ," but nevertheless insist that they...

> ...reject every kind of mystic union by which the faithful of Christ should in any way pass beyond the sphere of creatures and wrongly enter the divine, were it only to the extent of appropriating to themselves as their own but one single attribute of the eternal Godhead.[48]

However, while eternity is an attribute proper only to the Creator, Pius does not wish to exclude creatures from it, but only that they not presume to appropriate it "to themselves as their own."

In fact, a longing for eternity is inscribed within the very mystery of the human person, and by being grafted into the mystery of the Word made flesh that longing is fulfilled. Cardinal Darío Castrillón Hoyos beautifully restated this dynamic in his opening comments to a December, 2001 conference sponsored by the Vatican Congregation for the Clergy:

> The world needs transcendence, it longs to know and experience that human life is grafted into divine life. The sacraments of the New Covenant give man this capacity: to transcend what is limited and contingent, to be integrated in the immensity and eternity of God, and to recover 'the sacred meaning' of his own existence, by living a 'new life' of grace.

---

[48] *Mystici Corporis Christi*, 78.

Living in the divine will then emerges as a means by which man's fundamental longing for the divine eternity and immensity finds a more expanded field of fulfillment. While this field is on the one hand limited, that is, by the metaphysical parameters of his created nature and sanctifying grace, on the other hand it opens out to the infinite.

How man, in the divine will, can participate in past, present and future events.

Man's capacity, in the divine will, to contemplatively transcend his present historical moment and, by sharing in the eternal act of God, participate in events both before and after him, also needs to be seen within proper parameters. Even if man, by God's grace, can become present to all acts – past, present and future – this does not make him capable of changing completed history, or engaging in any other such nonsense associated with "time travel."

Rather, while remaining fully anchored to all the concrete dimensions of his present moment,[49] he yet also opens

---

[49] Divine will spirituality should not lead one to neglect the responsibilities, or devalue the significance, of life as one encounters it in the concrete, continuously unfolding present moment. Like any spirituality, if it is not grounded in the incarnational, it is merely the blowing of pious bubbles. But this need not happen as one attempts to live in the divine will. On the contrary, if one were to neglect or to devalue the concrete in a misguided pursuit of the abstract, he could be quite certain he was not living in the divine will at all, most especially because to do so would contradict the witness of Luisa's own life. Certainly she desired to be entirely hidden in Christ, but never to the neglect or devaluation of her ordinary, human and Christian

himself to all the unseen dimensions of that mystery – grounded in his identity as a transcendent creature made in God's image – by which he is connected to all creatures at all moments in time. Luisa writes:

> My poor mind was wandering in the immense sea of the Divine Fiat, in which everything is in act, as if there were no past and no future, but everything present and everything in act. So, whatever thing it wants to find of the works of its Creator in the Divine Will, my little soul finds it as if It were just doing it, in act.[50]

The soul who lives in the divine will still prays, feels and acts for his fellow man as he always has, but now within a far more widely expanded field of action, and in a far more connected sense. For example, he makes reparation for any sin that is being, has been or ever will be committed, and he does so in the very "moment" those sins are being committed. He likewise glorifies God for any good act that is being, has been or ever will be performed. He not only allows God, present within him by divinization, to fully take over his actions, but by his divinization he shares in that very act by which God divinizes all the baptized throughout time.

As with contemplative prayer, such acts in the divine will are not reducible to exercises that begin and end merely in man's imaginative and affective faculties. Rather, they are responses to authentic inner movements of the Spirit that are

---

responsibilities. Moving into the eternal moment is not an erasure of the present moment, but a radically deepened re-valuation of it.
[50] September 8, 1929, (26).

grounded in, and ordered toward, man's real ontological interconnectedness with God, his fellow man and all of creation.[51] God actually allows man to enter into his own eternal mode of being and operation, and therein not only gaze upon God with a deeper wonderment, but also exercise, with God, a real influence on the acts of each creature in the manner of preceding, accompanying and following them.

By assuming human nature, Christ established both the pattern and the means for man to act in this universal and "transtemporal" manner. Though he dwelt humanly within only a short span of history, by living every moment of it united with his divine will, he made himself present to all men at all times and moments of human history. And so, by the very act of his Incarnation, and in every human act that followed It, the Son of God eternally creates and redeems man. Luisa's diary proposes that God gave man, from the beginning, the capacity to join with him in a similar, eternal mode of action; through the redemption he restored that capacity; and through his revelation to Luisa he invites man to discover and live it anew.

---

[51] That man is actually, and not merely figuratively, capable of transcending his immediate concrete circumstances is proved by the manner in which he participates in the Eucharistic memorial of Christ's Passover. This sacrificial memorial or *anamnesis* "is not merely the recollection of past events but the proclamation of the mighty works wrought by God for men. In the liturgical celebration of these events they become in a certain way present and real." (CCC 1363) And because these events become in a certain way present and real to man, as man responds to them in faith, so does he in a certain way become present and real to them.

Man's reception of this gift, however, does not so much depend upon, and it certainly is not reducible to, his attaining a more refined grasp of the metaphysical relationship between time and eternity that Christ redeemed for him. Rather, it far more depends upon his continuous, authentic desire to see Christ's victory and his dominion reach every moment of created history and every corner of created existence, including, most especially, those moments and corners that would be utterly inaccessible to him apart from his union with God. To see that happen he must be willing to make his free will and all of his created talents disappear even more completely into God, and this requires him to journey even farther into the darkness of faith.

In short, man's reception of the gift of the divine will depends most especially upon radical humility and faith. Only upon such a platform is man able to see and utilize this gift for what it is: the most profound mode by which the humble, uncreated God generously allows the humble, created man to participate with him as he eternally pours out his infinite creativity and mercy.

How the human will unites with the divine will.

If Luisa's writings make it clear that the most perfect objective of a human act is to participate in God's own eternal act, they make it equally clear that that objective can be obtained only as the human will unites itself with the divine will in the most perfect manner. In various ways Jesus describes this as a union in which the two wills operate as if they were one. The human will not only conforms itself perfectly to the divine will, but is also in some sense "absorbed" into it.

As is typical of mystical literature, the language Luisa uses can seem exaggerated and even potentially problematic. However, if seen properly, her account not only conforms to the Church's mystical tradition but also sheds new light on the terminus of human perfection as it can be known in this life.

St. Paul describes the terminus of human perfection in simple, broad terms. It is that state in which the Christian can truly and in every sense say, "I live, no longer I, but Christ lives in me."[52] As a member of the body of Christ the Christian's union with Christ is as close as the Christian's union with the parts of his own body. Not only has he become, by baptism, "one body" with the Lord, but "whoever is joined to the Lord," Paul says, "becomes one spirit with him."[53]

This is not metaphorical language; it describes the reality. Spiritual progress is the journey toward its full actualization, and the paradox of the Gospel is the roadmap. And so it is in dying that we live, in losing that we gain, in becoming like a child that we mature, and so forth.

What this paradox says about the perfection of the human will, though, – and the associated perfection of human freedom and human dignity – is especially charged with irony. God calls the human will to perfect itself precisely along an axis of an ever more thorough, ever more consistent, immolation of itself, that is, for the sake of the divine will. Thus, the more completely we relinquish to God

---

[52] Gal 2:20
[53] I Cor. 6:17.

our freedom, that is, to live apart from him, the more truly free we become. The more thoroughly we strip ourselves of our human pride, the more dignity of our divine sonship we discover. The more we detach ourselves from all that is not the Creator himself, the more capable we become of fulfilling our destiny as creatures made in his image.

Heavenly beatitude, of course, stands as the ultimate terminus of this journey of the human will. But what is its terminus in this life? The Church's mystical tradition describes it as a co-operative union between the human will and the divine will that is so close that the two can be said to constitute two principles of one action. What is human becomes so overwhelmed, so engulfed by what is divine, that the soul perceives its union with God as its utter annihilation, the elimination even of its ability to act at all. St. John of the Cross describes it in compelling terms:

> Thus in this state the soul cannot make acts because the Holy Spirit makes them all and moves it toward them. As a result all the acts of the soul are divine, since the movement toward these acts and their execution stems from God. Hence it seems to a person that every time this flame shoots up, making him love with delight and divine quality, it is giving him eternal life, since it raises him up to the activity of God in God.[54]

> This union resembles the union of the light of a star or candle with the light of the sun, for what then sheds light is not the star or the candle, but the sun, which

---

[54] St. John of the Cross, *The Living Flame of Love*, Stanza 1, Paragraph 4.

has absorbed the other lights into its own... The union wrought between the two natures and the communication of the divine to the human in this state is such that even though neither changes its being, both appear to be God.[55]

When St. John says that the soul in this state of union "cannot make acts" he does not mean that the human will has been disabled. On the contrary, this domination by the divine will takes place only so long as the human will continuously allows it. Rather, in this state the soul perceives with an intense clarity the reality of St. Paul's words: "It is God who works in you to will and to act according to his good purpose." (Phil. 2:13)[56]

The soul, for example, sees that it is ultimately God who resists sin within the soul's victories over temptation; it is God who cares for the poor through the soul's works of mercy.[57] While the human will remains involved in each of these good decisions, the soul perceives what has in fact been the reality all along, that is, that his will is capable of making only one good decision that has its origin in his created nature,[58] and that is to "disappear" in order that God might have his full dominion through and within the soul.

_____

[55] St. John of the Cross, *The Spiritual Canticle,* Stanza 22, Paragraphs 3 & 4.
[56] C.f., Is. 26:12, "It is you who have accomplished all that we have done," and Mt. 10:20, "It will not be you who speak, but the Spirit of your Father speaking through you."
[57] In this way the soul more and more reflects the life and mind of Jesus who in all things yielded to the Father's will and who acknowledged that "the Father who dwells in me is doing his works." (Jn. 14:10.)
[58] Even this decision, however, can only be made in response to the promptings of grace and with its assistance.

Bringing this traditional understanding of mystical "absorption" to Luisa's writings is essential for properly interpreting what Jesus tells her about how the human will operates in the divine will. He says, for instance:

> Now, for one who... lives in my Divine will, the human volition ceases, its life ends, nor has any reason to exist any longer, because the life of the unity of my Will begins.[59]

> When I enter in a soul and find her will, her desires, her affections, her thoughts, and her heart all Mine, I absorb her in Me; and with the fire of my Love I liquefy her will in Mine, and make of them one alone. I liquefy her desires in Mine, her affection and her thoughts in Mine.[60]

This is dramatic and potentially problematic language, but the greater context of Luisa's life and literature makes clear that the human will remains ontologically intact. Far from it eliminating or debilitating the human will, living in the divine will depends upon a continuous, dynamic, synergistic relationship between the human and divine wills. Jesus explains:

> My daughter, in the union of Our Wills, all will be enclosed. Your will will operate alongside of Mine in beseeching graces for the salvation of souls.[61]

---

[59] November 14, 1928, (25).
[60] June 7, 1917, (12).
[61] August 12, 1915, (11).

Is it not wonderful that the flowing of a human will can be in constant relationship with a Divine Will and that one can have its outlet in the other?[62]

When the human will unites with the Divine Will, the two wills embrace and repose together.[63]
(God and the creature) are two beings clasped together, inseparable, transfused, identified, such that it can barely be recognized that they are two lives palpitating together.[64]

And so, as the soul enters into the divine will, the "absorption" of the human will can be and must be understood as it has always been understood in the Catholic mystical tradition, that is, not as an act contrary to its perfection, but as a precondition for it. But if this is true, another question arises.

Distinguishing living in the divine will from the mystical tradition

If the operations of the human will are to be understood within the parameters of the mystical tradition, what greater perfection could they possibly obtain by entering into the divine will? Has the human will not already reached the terminus of its perfection, for example, as St. John describes it above?

---

[62] March 16, 1922, (14).
[63] March 18, 1922, (14).
[64] January 25, 1927, (20).

Jesus answers this question in various ways, and often uses the sun as an illustration. For instance, in the following passage[65] he describes four people participating in the life of the sun, each representing a different degree of living in the divine will.[66] The first is like a person in a room. Only a small amount of light enters and no heat. The second person goes outside and enjoys more light and feels the heat of the sun's rays. The third person, who represents mystical union as it has been traditionally experienced, positions himself where…

>…the solar rays hit the surface of the earth. This one feels invested by its rays, he feels burned by the heat of the sun; the vividness of its light is such that, his eyes being filled with it, he can hardly look at the earth. He sees himself as though transfused, one could say, into the very light; he feels little of the earth, of himself, and only because he has his feet on the ground, but he lives only for the sun… (He) is the image of one who has advanced into the boundaries of this Kingdom; and Its light is such and so great as to make him forget everything. He no longer feels anything of himself; good, virtues, crosses, change into his own nature; the light eclipses him, transforms

---

[65] July 26, 1926, (19).

[66] It is noteworthy that in this particular diary entry, Jesus employs the term "living in the divine will" in a broad sense, that is, to include anyone who participates in the life of God. In so doing, Jesus does not characterize the spirituality he introduces to and through Luisa as a fundamentally new order of union with God, but rather as a new degree. This helps to reinforce the continuity of Luisa's spirituality with the Catholic Tradition. I will explore this crucial issue further in the following section, "The Third Fiat of God."

him, and just barely allows him to look from afar at what no longer belongs to him.

The fourth person represents the new spirituality Jesus introduces to and through Luisa. This person…

> …takes flight into the solar rays, and rises up to the center of its sphere. This one remains burned by the intensity of the heat that the sun contains in its center; the intensity of the light eclipses him completely, in such a way that he remains dissolved, consumed, within the sun itself. This fourth person can no longer look at the earth nor think of himself; and if he does look, he will look at light, he will feel fire. So, for him all things have ended; light and heat have taken the place of his life… (He) is the happiest, because he is the image of one who not only lives in my Kingdom, but has acquired It. This one undergoes the total consummation in the Supreme Sun of my Will; the eclipse caused by Its light is so intense, that he himself becomes light and heat, nor can he look at anything else but light and fire; and all things convert for him into light and love.

We might still wonder how the experience of this fourth person differs all that much, or at all, from that of St. John of the Cross, who perceives having been raised up "to the activity of God in God," and who indeed appears, to himself, to be God. Of course we cannot make precise comparisons here, because we are not comparing the actual core subjective experiences, but only the descriptions of them, and those descriptions, by the testimony of the writers themselves, do not and cannot adequately capture their experiences. However, to the extent that we can fairly enter into St. John's and Luisa's respective subjective experiences, there do appear to be some differences.

St. John, for instance, does not seem to demonstrate the same awareness or intention that Luisa had of participating in all of God's creative and redemptive work across the span of created history and existence. Certainly this is not to say that he would have resisted such a participation, but it could be that God, in his good pleasure, had not yet deemed to extend to the creature that particular dimension of being a participant in the divine nature.

As compared to the traditional accounts of mystical union, Luisa's also more closely looks to, and mirrors, the mode in which the human will operated in man's original innocence. While it is not novel to look upon the state of man's original innocence, and especially the original state of his will,[67] as a fundamental norm for Christian perfection, it would appear that Luisa's account lifts our sights to a new height. Jesus speaks, for example, of the soul in the divine will regaining the full glory of her original boundlessness, that is, to "freely wander within her God, throughout the heavens."[68] He explains further:

---

[67] In his book, *From Death to Life: The Christian Journey* (Ignatius Press, San Francisco: 1995), p. 50, Cardinal (then Bishop) Christoph Schönborn reinforces the patristic tradition that looks upon man's original dignity, most especially with respect to his human will, as the fundamental norm of his restoration in Christ: "Deification is located in the reestablishing of fallen man in his innate dignity. If it is clear that the fall was caused by a perversion of the human will, then it follows that the reestablishing must affect above all the act of human willing."

[68] April 14, 1927, (21).

And since it is Divine Will that flows, it disposes the creature to ask for Its Kingdom, and We feel that the creature who lives in Our Divine Will calls back the feasts, the amusements, the games of the beginning of Creation with her Creator. Everything is licit for one who lives in Our Will, and We let her do everything, because she wants nothing but Our Will and Our echo which resounds in her. Letting herself be carried by Our divine echo, now she throws her little rock, now she forms her little wind which now forms the waves, now moans, now speaks, now prays that it wants Our Divine Fiat to be known and loved, and to dominate over the earth.[69]

Living in the divine will does not restore to our nature all the pristine effects of man's original, innocent unity with God. It is, rather, a new, "living form"[70] of that original unity, to which God calls us to lay claim. Though we remain wounded by sin, we are nevertheless elevated by and in Christ to all the fullness of our original dignity, which

---

[69] September 5, 1928, (24). Passages like this should allay any concerns that Luisa, in promoting such an extreme form of passivity before the divine will, might be promoting a new form of Quietism. Far from aiming for that lifeless, inactive, and ultimately amoral resignation characteristic of Quietism, divine will spirituality aims rather for a dynamic activity directed entirely for God's glory.

[70] John Paul II summarizes the proper sense in which we, "historical man," are to look back upon "original man" and discover a deeper sense of who we might become again: "Christ does not invite man to return to the state of original innocence, because humanity has irrevocably left it behind, but He calls him to rediscover – on the foundation of the perennial and, so to speak, indestructible meanings of what is 'human' – the living forms of the 'new man.'" General Audience, December 3, 1980, as reported in L'Osservatore Romano, December 9, 1980.

includes the dignity of relating to God in the same fundamental manner in which Adam and Eve related to him in the beginning. Luisa's account, vis a vis the mystical tradition, does appear to show that God has opened up a new vista into that original, and ultimate, manner of relating to him. Because the effects of sin linger within and around us, we may not be able to perceive the vast scope of the beauties, harmonies and effects of that unity as profoundly and palpably as man did before the fall. But that does not render our participation any less real or any less pleasing to God.

Study and Reflection Questions

1. Obedience to rightful authority and humility are among those basics of the spiritual life that are prerequisite to any experience of mystical union with God. Why are these two qualities especially indispensable to living in the divine will?

2. What are some of the other basics of the spiritual life, and how can their practice be expanded and elevated through living in the divine will?

3. Christians have always been called and empowered by the Holy Spirit to restore to creation all its original value. Luisa's writings suggest that God now wants us to expand those restorative efforts to reach across all of time and space. How is this possible? What differences, if any, would this mean in terms of how we live our everyday lives?

4. "Grace is *participation in the life of God*. It introduces us into the intimacy of Trinitarian life." (CCC 1997, emphasis in the original). If living in the divine will is a new gift that God is only now giving to the Church, it is crucial to understand it as new only in *degree*, that is, as an eternally expanded experience and expression of grace, and not as new in *essence*, that is, as something separate and different from grace. Why is this distinction so important?

5. If living in the divine will is indeed the highest expression of intimacy with God that is possible in this life, it is so because – and only because – it is also associated with the most intimate embrace of our ordinary and Christian responsibilities that is possible in this life. Explain why living in intimacy with God and embracing our human responsibilities are absolutely interconnected.

III.

THE THIRD FIAT OF GOD

Overview

Throughout the long record of Luisa's mystical experiences, Jesus told her that living in the divine will is the highest state of union with God that can be known in this life. It is the state that man enjoyed in his original innocence, that he lost through his own fault, and that God, in the fullness of time and in his mercy and generosity, fully restored to man. First, by a singular grace, he made the Virgin Mary, from the first moment of her Immaculate Conception, to be the first person to live once again in the divine will. Her fiat established the "first link" by which all mankind was to be restored to this state. Subsequently, through the Incarnation and redemption, Christ also not only lived in the divine will himself, but fully regained man's right and ability to enjoy that state again.

However, even though Jesus definitively restored man's right and ability to live in the divine will, until Luisa only Jesus and his mother *actually* lived in that state, even far beyond the measure that Adam and Eve had lived in it in the beginning. Jesus told Luisa that by a singular privilege she had been called to be the first person since Mary and himself to live in that state again. In other words, in the two thousand-year history of the Church, no saint, no matter how close his or her union with God, had ever enjoyed this degree of union. To Luisa's bewilderment, Jesus explained that not until her did he consider it opportune to make known and bestow this most exalted fruit of the redemption, not only for her sake but for the sake of the entire Church. As if this were not astonishing enough, Jesus added even more.

Jesus told Luisa that though she had been born into humanity's common stock of original sin, she had been elected by God to serve the role of a "second virgin." By accepting his invitation to live in the divine will she would offer her own "fiat," thus forming a "second link" that would, in some sense, be necessary for the ultimate accomplishment of his universal plan. That is, as she and others following her lead would live in the divine will again, they would become the means by which God would ultimately draw his works of creation and redemption to their historical conclusion and fulfillment.

Jesus characterizes this process – his revelation to Luisa about this new gift of mystical union, her accepting it, her living in it and her passing knowledge of it on to others so that they too can live it – as the "third fiat" of God. It is thus characterized in Luisa's writings as the means by which God, in man, will "complete" his first and second fiats.

His first fiat was the fiat of creation. God willed that man and the universe come into being, and that man thereafter fulfill God's will in everything. As the lord of creation, man was to continuously do each of his acts, exterior and interior, in the divine will, and thereby make God's will and glory fully regnant in every corner and moment of created existence. By his disobedience man separated himself from the divine will and could not return to it by his own efforts. Not only did he set himself upon an ineluctable course toward eternal separation from God, but because he could no longer do his acts in the divine will, he also lost his ability to accomplish God's original plan for the universe.

Moreover, since he was to have done, but could no longer do, each of his acts in the divine will, the gulf between God's initial, perfect plan for man and the sad reality of man's actual condition has grown ever wider since that original sin. That is, with each successive act of each successive human creature that has not been done in the divine will – even good and otherwise holy acts – the aggregate deficit of man's due response to God has grown larger. Since the ultimate fulfillment of God's plan for man and the universe still, even after the fall, depended upon man's response in the divine will, it became necessary for God himself to do that work for man, as a man.

God completed this work by his second fiat, the fiat of redemption. By his life, death and resurrection, the Son of God not only saved man from eternal separation from God, he also made up for every act of every man not done in the divine will. Thus, in Christ, the gulf between God and man was completely closed, and the deficit of man's due response to God in the divine will was completely erased. God thereby entirely reconciled man and the world to himself.

Jesus told Luisa, however, that even though God's work, first in creating man and then in redeeming him, was fully completed by Christ, it yet remains man's right and responsibility to make God's work fully manifest. Indeed,

God's plan for man and the universe cannot and will not be consummated until man fully responds to God in this same manner that Christ did. In other words, to fulfill God's work of creation and redemption it remains necessary for man – through, with and in Christ – to live as Christ did and as Adam and Eve did in the beginning, that is, by doing (and reparatively re-doing) all of his acts in the divine will. This is what God's third fiat – given to man through Luisa – will accomplish.

The context of this evaluation

In writing about a new holiness and a third fiat, Luisa had neither the intention nor the wherewithal to propose and defend a new theological view about how God will consummate his plans for man and the universe. She was a woman of minimal education who wrote not to offer her own thoughts about anything, but only to provide, out of obedience, a record of what Jesus told her. Neither did she write about Jesus choosing her for a singular role in effecting God's designs because of any of her own desires or delusions of grandiosity. On the contrary, she was obviously an otherwise entirely hidden woman who was embarrassed about this election and reluctant to record anything about it. She did so, again, only because she was ordered to. In short, even though Luisa might have expected a theological scrutiny of her writings, it is clear that she did nothing on her own initiative to invite it.

Nevertheless, such theological scrutiny is most certainly necessary, especially with respect to all that surrounds these notions of a new holiness, a third fiat and Luisa's singular role in effecting them. Nothing in Sacred Scripture nor

Tradition creates an expectation that between the redemption and Christ's return in glory there would be any such intermediate, universal divine initiative, moreover, one coming by way of a new revelation to a divinely selected human mediator. Indeed divine Revelation might seem to indicate that we are *not* to expect such an initiative.

Therefore, all that is proposed in Luisa's writings about a third fiat comes, at the minimum, as a surprise to the Church.[71] Before it can be allowed into the body of authentic Christian literature it must be seen either to advance, to support, or at least not to contradict, the essential principles and aims of divine Revelation.

In what follows I offer such an interpretation. I should acknowledge at the outset that this interpretation is not self-evident in the original form of Luisa's literature. But neither is it inconsistent with anything she wrote. On the contrary, I derive this interpretation entirely from thematic threads that run throughout her literature, even if, in their original form, they were not so purposefully arranged and explicated to correspond to Catholic teaching.

My objective in interpreting these themes in this manner is not to alter, correct or superimpose meaning upon them, but only to identify their inner arc and follow that arc toward its objective. And it is clear to me that the central objective of Jesus' revelation to Luisa is not to introduce anything

---

[71] Jesus acknowledged this, and in fact expressed a measure of delight about it. He told Luisa, "I want to give this surprise to the human generations – the Kingdom of my Divine Will on earth; a surprise not expected by them." May 31, 1929, (26).

essentially new to divine Revelation, but only to call man to a greater holiness that will both represent and hasten the ultimate coming of the Kingdom of God's will.

Moreover, Jesus would have man respond to this call only in harmony with the call he has already made to man through the certain and everlasting authority of divine Revelation. Jesus insists that no opposition should be seen between his revelation to Luisa and what has been made manifest in Sacred Scripture:

> Now, that which I manifest on my Divine Will, and which you write, can be called 'the Gospel of the Kingdom of the Divine Will'. In nothing does it oppose either Sacred Scriptures (i.e., the Old Testament) or the Gospel which I announced while being on earth; on the contrary, It can be called the support of one and of the other.[72]

Of course, for Jesus to claim that his revelation to Luisa supports divine Revelation is no proof that it does. But the greater context within which Luisa received his revelation makes it clear that she not only would have welcomed collateral proofs of its continuity with divine Revelation, but in fact she would have considered such proofs to be essential to the entire project.[73] And so I offer this interpretation of the third fiat of God trusting that I am serving the Servant of God's innermost intentions.

---

[72] January 18, 1928, (23).
[73] I develop this point earlier in the section, *Luisa's Obedience: the Key to her Life, Writings and Spirituality*

Situating the third fiat within the paradox by which Christ's definitive Revelation is both complete and not yet completed.

A review of the theological structures of public and private revelation provides a useful point to begin evaluating Luisa's revelation about a third fiat of God.

When the unseen God revealed himself two thousand years ago in the flesh of Jesus Christ, his self-revelation was complete and definitive – as was his work in redeeming man. Nothing more remained for God to reveal or to accomplish that would be essential to man's salvation and growth in holiness. The associated body or "deposit" of revealed truth that the Apostles received, and in turn handed on to all generations, is what we have come to know as "public Revelation."

Because it is complete, "…no new public revelation is to be expected before the glorious manifestation of our Lord, Jesus Christ."[74] Knowing this to be true, Christians of every age have been assured that the Church offers them in word and in sacrament all that God wishes to give man for his salvation and sanctification:

> Everything we need for holiness and increase in faith has been handed on from the Apostles once and for all. What was handed on by the apostles comprises everything that serves to make the People of God live their lives in holiness and increase their faith.[75]

[74] *Dei Verbum*, 4.
[75] *Dei Verbum*, 8.

There is, however, a fundamental paradox to the completeness of God's self-revelation: "Yet even if Revelation is already complete, it has not been made completely explicit; it remains for Christian faith gradually to grasp its full significance over the course of the centuries."[76] It is a paradox rooted in the central paradox of the coming of the kingdom in the Gospels, where the immanence of the kingdom revealed in the person of Jesus is always held in tension with the transcendence of the kingdom yet to come in its fullness.

Cognizant of this tension, the Church has believed for two thousand years that even while she is the custodian of the fullness of divine truth, she herself has not yet reached the "plenitude of divine truth." She thus proclaims the Word of God anew to every generation, while she yet awaits the "fulfillment" of that same Word within her:

> The Tradition that comes from the apostles makes progress in the Church, with the help of the Holy Spirit. There is growth in insight into the realities and words that are being passed on. This comes about in various ways... Thus, as the centuries go by, the Church is always advancing towards the plenitude of divine truth, until eventually the words of God are fulfilled in her.[77]

It is in serving this paradox that private revelation finds a limited, but nonetheless divinely ordained purpose. Since God has already, once and for all, revealed himself in Christ to all generations, it is not the role of any private revelation "to

---

[76] CCC 66.
[77] *Dei Verbum*, 8.

improve or complete Christ's definitive Revelation, but to help live more fully by it in a certain period of history."[78] In other words, so long as a private revelation does not presume to add to or subtract from the substance of public Revelation, it may advance the aims of public Revelation.

Private revelation can even be viewed as one of those "various ways" by which the Spirit leads the Church to that "growth in insight into the realities and words that are being passed on." Private revelation can thus contribute to the eventual fulfillment of the words of God in the Church.[79]

St. John of the Cross could be said to summarize the legitimate role of private revelation in serving the paradox of Christ's definitive Revelation. While he strenuously warned against any private revelation that claims to reveal new and secret mysteries, he yet welcomed insights of any kind that could help the Church better appreciate the wonders that God revealed to man in Christ, and accomplished for man in Christ:

> ...however numerous are the mysteries and marvels which holy doctors have discovered and saintly souls understood in this earthly life, all the more is yet to be said and understood. There is much to fathom in Christ, for He is like an abundant mine with many recesses of treasures, so that however deep men go

---

[78] CCC 67.

[79] In Cardinal Joseph Ratzinger's "Theological Commentary In Preparation for the Release of the Third Part of the Secret of Fatima" (L'Osservatore Romano, June 28, 2000) he submits that private revelation can fit within the meaning of these words of Dei Verbum, 8.

they never reach the end or bottom, but rather in every recess find new veins with new riches everywhere.[80]

This paradox within which Christ's definitive Revelation is both complete but not yet completed forms the foundation for evaluating the claims made in Luisa's private revelation about a third fiat, a new holiness and so forth.

Thus, so long as her revelation does not purport to improve or complete divine truth, but only to assist the Church in "advancing toward the plenitude of divine truth,"[81] it stays within the limits of authentic private revelation, and can serve a useful role. Is this the case for her revelation?

In the following excerpts we see that while Jesus affirms that his work in creation and redemption is complete and therefor not in need of supplementation, he also affirms that the work of these first two Fiats is not yet completed. He is issuing the third fiat to serve that aim:

> My daughter, everything was made in Creation. In It, the Divinity manifested all Its Majesty, Power and Wisdom, and displayed His complete Love toward

---

[80] St. John of the Cross, *The Spiritual Canticle*, Stanza 37, paragraph 4.

[81] It is true that the "advancement" Luisa describes in her diary is not explicitly ordered toward a fulfillment or completion of God's *words*, but rather of his *deeds*, i.e., his works of redemption and creation. And yet the inner, divine logic of his words and his deeds is identical and inseparable. That is, his self-revelation is manifested in both his words and his deeds. They share an inner unity and in fact constitute a single reality. (*Dei Verbum*, 2 - 4) Thus, it is not only God's words but also his works which are continuously advancing toward their plenitude in the Church. To advance one is necessarily to advance the other.

the creatures. There is not one point, either in Heaven or on earth, or in any created thing, in which the perfection of Our Works is not complete. Not one thing was left half-made. In Creation, God showed off all His works for the creatures; He loved with complete love, and made complete works – there was nothing to be added or to be removed. So, I made everything perfect; nor can We do incomplete works; on the contrary, in each created thing We placed a distinct and complete love in Creation, for each creature.[82]

Now the completion of the work of Creation was that man should fulfill our Will in everything. This was to be the Life, the food, the crown of the creature; but since this is not yet the case, the work of Creation is not yet complete; and neither can I repose in it nor it in Me.[83]

It is only because my Humanity lived in the center of the Divine Will that I was able to encompass all in a single act. I was thus able to complete the work of Redemption in a manner befitting Myself. Had it been otherwise, the work of Redemption would have been incomplete and unworthy of Myself.[84]

My daughter, all my works are complete. Thus the glory that the creature should give Me will be complete, and the last day will not come if all creation

---

[82] June 3, 1925, (17).
[83] September 11, 1922, (14).
[84] October 19, 1922, (14).

does not give Me the honor and glory desired and established by Me.[85]

The plan of Redemption and that of the "Fiat Voluntas Tua," as in Heaven so on earth, would not have been worthy of Me if I had not rehabilitated man, in everything, as he was created. He would have been a work done in half measure – incomplete – and your Jesus does not know how to do incomplete work.[86]

And I, coming upon the earth, had to do as a God; I had to complete in everything the work of man; I had to raise him to the first point of his origin, by giving him the possession of my Will. And, although many make use of my Coming as remedy for their salvation, and therefore take my Will as medicine, as strength, as antidote in order to not go to Hell, I still wait so that souls rise who will take It as Life; and, in making It known, they take possession of It. In this way I will complete the work of my Coming upon the earth and will have the fruit of the Divine Graft formed anew with the creature, and my tears will be changed into Celestial and Divine smiles for Me and for them.[87]

Thus, God's work in creating and redeeming man is characterized as complete, while man's work – to make manifest the effects of God's work – yet remains incomplete:

---

[85] May 22, 1919, (12).
[86] November 10, 1923, (16).
[87] December 20, 1925, (18).

"My daughter, all that has been done by Our Divinity, both in Creation and in Redemption, has not all been absorbed by the creature, but is all in my Divine Will, in waiting, to give itself to creatures."[88] This is why Jesus is initiating the third fiat: to dramatically assist man in fully responding to God.

The third fiat understood as a catalyst

With this "complete though not yet completed" paradox in mind, perhaps the best way to characterize the third fiat is as a catalyst. God's previous, fully complete, creative and redemptive initiatives have been continuously at work within the Church, gradually moving her toward her earthly fulfillment. The Church knows that the Spirit, moving within her in various and sometimes unexpected ways, will eventually complete this work. But she does not know exactly how or when.

Given this uncertainty, the Church could allow for the third fiat so long as it is understood only as a means that God has unexpectedly introduced to rapidly accelerate the already active process by which his already complete first and second fiats have been gradually reaching their historical completion in and through man.

Such a view allows the third fiat to be paradoxically both categorized, and not categorized, with the first and second fiats. That is, Christians could choose if they will[89] to view

---

[88] October 28, 1928. (25).

[89] Because anything the Church might know about a third fiat of God comes to her only by way of Luisa's private revelation, Christians must not, and indeed they cannot, give it the assent of religious faith. But this does not necessarily mean that God is not inviting the entire Church to assent to

the third fiat in the same conceptual category as the first and second fiats, that is, as a singular divine initiative manifested at the universal level. But they would view it in this way only because they simultaneously view it in a conceptual category entirely distinguishable from the previous two. That is, the effects of the third fiat, unlike the effects of the first and second fiats, do not originate from that fiat itself. Rather, because this third divine initiative operates only as a catalyst, all effects that might flow from it originate entirely from the two precedent divine initiatives.[90]

And so, however troublesome the notion of a consummating third fiat might appear at first, God is, by means of it, doing nothing more than releasing effects (i.e., actualizing potencies) that he has already definitively dispensed by means of his first two fiats.[91]

---

it, although, of course, with only human faith (i.e., the response of right reason) and not with religious faith. The Church has already approved many other private revelations through which God similarly asked for a universal response from the Church, e.g., Jesus' revelations about his Sacred Heart to St. Margaret Mary, and his Divine Mercy to St. Faustina.

[90] In chemistry a catalyst is defined as a substance that initiates or accelerates a chemical reaction without itself being consumed in the process. In other words, it only provides the occasion for a new release of energy from the reactants; it is not the origin of that energy.

[91] Similarly, any authority Luisa's revelation might possess as a revelation into the mystery of God would not flow from its own inner light but from the unique, descriptive penetration it would provide into the light of the Gospel. Just as it is the sun and not the magnifying glass that ignites the dry leaf, so it is Christ's definitive Revelation and not Luisa's private revelation that ignites the hearts of the faithful in a new way.

This distinction is crucial for properly understanding a certain sub-theme that runs through Luisa's revelation. On several occasions Jesus characterizes the work of the third fiat not only as conceptually comparable to God's previous work in the first and second fiats, but as the *greater* work. For instance, in a letter to Saint Annibale, Luisa describes God's mission in the third fiat as, "in the very words of Jesus, '...more important than the very creation and redemption, because it will be the fulfillment of both one and the other'."[92]

Such comments must, of course, be interpreted with great care. But the dominant sense that emerges from her literature is not that Jesus would have us favorably compare the mission of the third fiat as against the missions of the first and second, that is, as if it were distinguishable from them. Rather, he compares the former phase of those two divine missions with their latter phase.

In the former phase, God created and redeemed man and these two divine works first began to show their effects in and through man. In their latter phase, God will finally make manifest, again in and through man, the most profound effects of those two divine works. If the latter, "post third fiat" phase, can be said to be greater than the former, "pre third fiat" phase, it is only in the sense that it will witness a greater manifestation of effects that proceed

---

[92] Letter from Luisa to Father Annibale, 22 October 1926, Archives of the Rogationist Postulation (Rome), [Archivio Postulazione Rogazionisti - Roma] Inventory No. 5875.

from the same essential and continuous works of creation and redemption.[93]

Properly understanding Luisa's fiat and revelation as "necessary" for the full accomplishment of God's work in creation and redemption.

But viewing the third fiat analogously as a catalyst that "completes" God's works of creation and redemption by dramatically drawing forth their effects does not answer all questions that Christian doctrine poses. What is to be done with the claim that through Luisa's fiat and private revelation God is unveiling a new expression of holiness – one that has neither been known nor experienced by anyone other than Jesus and Mary, moreover, one that will finally allow man to accomplish his original, God-given mission for the universe?

Do not such claims improperly elevate her fiat and her private revelation by making them a necessary condition for the full accomplishment of the era of salvation? Do these claims not imply that reaching this degree of sanctity would have been impossible before and without Luisa and her private revelation? Furthermore, how can we think that Jesus would have kept *anything*, much less the very pinnacle of holiness,

---

[93] In his farewell discourse, Jesus makes what appears to be a similar comparison: "Amen, amen, I say to you, whoever believes in me will do the works that I do, and will do greater ones than these, because I am going to the Father." (Jn. 14:12) The Lord does not favorably compare his disciples' work against his own, as if their work could be considered distinguishable from his. Rather, he portrays the works that his disciples will do both as an extension of his own works and as a manifestation of them greater even than what has already been made manifest, that is, during the earthly phase of his life.

"hidden" from his Church and his saints these past two thousand years?

We can begin addressing these questions by considering the relationship between the Church's progress in her knowledge of divine Revelation and her progress in holiness. To recall, as the Church moves through the centuries she is "always advancing towards the plenitude of divine truth, until eventually the words of God are fulfilled in her."[94] But what sort of fulfillment of God's words is the Church ultimately expecting? It is more than merely a perfected intellectual grasp of the words of God:

> "Faith *seeks understanding*": it is intrinsic to faith that a believer desires to know better the One in whom he has put his faith and to understand better what He has revealed; a more penetrating knowledge will in turn call forth a greater faith, increasingly set afire by love.[95]

As it is true for the individual believer, so it is true for the Church: her ever-deepening penetration into the mysteries of divine Revelation is ordered toward her loving Christ ever more fully, and thereby growing in holiness. The Church thus looks back to her origin knowing that she has always been holy, and yet she also looks forward expecting that she will, in some true sense, become holier still. That is, guided and strengthened by the Spirit, she will grow unto the fullness of her knowledge of, and love for, Christ.

---

[94] *Dei Verbum*, 8.
[95] CCC 158, emphasis in original.

The Lord's revelation to Luisa serves this dynamic. It discloses new insights into what Christ has accomplished for man that are ordered toward helping the Church advance closer to the plenitude of divine truth and thus advance toward the plenitude of holiness. It could even be allowed that by means of this revelation he is helping the Church better perceive and aspire to the very highest possible form of sanctity. But none of this need imply that Luisa's fiat or her revelation is a necessary condition for Christians to attain this highest form of sanctity, or for the Church to fulfill her mission "to sum up all things in Christ."[96] An analogy might help to illustrate this point.

By way of a simple equation, $E = MC^2$, Albert Einstein, in 1905, described forces of energy in the universe that were not only greater than what man had known before, but greater than what man had even imagined. Moreover, these vast new reservoirs of energy could be found in the minutest particles of matter. But perhaps what is most remarkable about his discovery is that it was nothing more than the first statement of a truth that had always been true.

Was he the first human to see it? Perhaps. But even if his "private revelation" about energy-mass equivalence might have been the first *occasion* of its becoming known, it does not necessarily follow that his revelation was the necessary *condition* for its becoming known. Simply put, it could have become known in and through anyone before him. Likewise, nuclear energy had never been "impossible" for man to perceive and utilize before Einstein.

---

[96] Eph. 1:10.

In a similar sense the Church can understand Luisa's revelation about how man can live in the divine will and thereby accomplish God's plan for the universe. As man has always possessed all the treasures of the material universe, the Church has always possessed all the treasures of divine Revelation. As scientists ponder the universe in order that man might ever more fully mine material treasures, the Church ponders the mysteries of Revelation in order that man might ever more fully mine divine treasures. As Einstein helps man discover a vast, surprisingly new dimension of his material inheritance, Luisa helps the Church discover a vast, surprisingly new dimension of her divine inheritance. And, as to both Einstein and Luisa, it would not have been impossible for someone before them to have seen what they saw for the first time. But it would have been impossible for either of them, or for anyone else, to have seen what they saw before God inspired them to see it.

Before continuing with this analogy I should offer two qualifications.

First, by linking the Church's pondering of the mysteries of divine Revelation to the mining of divine treasures I do not mean to imply that the Church's ever-expanding deposit of objective knowledge (to which Luisa's revelation would contribute) establishes some sort of ever-expanding outer limit of possible sanctity in her members. Every gift of sanctity, including the gift of living in the divine will, has been the heritage of *every* Christian in *every* generation. "Blessed be the God and Father of our Lord Jesus Christ, who has blessed us in Christ with every spiritual blessing in the heavens."[97] "He who did not spare his own Son but handed him over for us all, how will he not also give us everything else along with him?"[98]

The fact that the Spirit continuously and in various ways reveals new depths of insight to the Church only demonstrates God's desire to help the Church better appropriate the divine treasures of sanctity; it does not imply that former generations had only lower possibilities of sanctity available to them. And so, even if Luisa's account of living in the divine will describes the most advanced form of mystical union that is possible in this life, her account is given only to help others attain it, not to imply that it would have been impossible for those before her to have enjoyed it as well, that is, if God had so willed it.

Second, God extends these new insights to and through Luisa not merely to draw forth a more profound marvel and assent of man's intellect, but principally to inspire a more profound conversion of his heart. Jesus tells Luisa,

> It is not enough to have the will to know the truths if, at the light of the truth which illuminates him, one does not try to dust himself of his own weaknesses, reorder himself according to the light of the truth he knows, and put himself to work together with the light of truth, making of it his own substance, in such a way that the light of the truth which he has absorbed may shine forth from his mouth, from his hands, from his bearing. It would be as if he killed the

---

[97] Eph. 1:3.
[98] Rom. 8:32.

truth; and by not putting it into practice, it would be like remaining in total disorder before the light.[99]

By insisting that living in the divine will demands an obedience of both mind and will, that is, an assent marked by both faith and works, Jesus insists that the "new knowledge" he reveals to Luisa not be perceived as a neo-Gnosticism.[100] That Luisa understood this is made clear as much by the heroic witness of her life as it is in her writings. The point was re-iterated by her extraordinary confessor, Saint Annibale di Francia: "I always insist on one point, and that is this: sanctity does not consist of a formula. With this new Science, in order to form Saints who surpass the ones of the past, it is important that the new Saints possess all the virtues to a heroic degree, just as did the Saints of old…"[101]

With these two qualifications in mind, the point I wish to make by this analogy to Einstein's discovery is that God's initiative is the necessary condition for the manifestation of this new outpouring of sanctity, not Luisa's fiat or the new insights of her private revelation. They might be the first

---

[99] November 19, 1921, (13).

[100] This recurrent heresy characteristically locates salvation in the mere possession of an arcane knowledge of the mysteries of the universe and in an associated series of occult formulas.

[101] *Collection of Letters Sent by Blessed Father Annibale de Francia to The Servant of God Luisa Piccarreta* (Jacksonville, FL: The Center for the Divine Will, 1997) p. 9. What St. Annibale says about the importance of heroic virtue should be understood in a balanced sense. Those of us who wish to live in the divine will but who are not yet living a life of heroic virtue should not be discouraged, but neither should we be complacent. God alone will lift us in time to the heights of holiness and heroic virtue, but only if we continuously and genuinely show him through our lives that we truly desire to get there.

occasion of this new manifestation, but they are not its cause. So long as we believe, i.e., with religious faith, that at any time before Luisa, Christ *could* have manifested to anyone else the degree of union that she experienced and described, we are free to suppose, i.e., believe with human faith, that in fact he did not.[102]

But even if it must be said that it is the Lord's initiative and not Luisa's private revelation that is the necessary condition for this new blossoming of faith, this does not mean that her "fiat" in response to his initiative could not have its own proper, secondary sense of being necessary. Such was the case with the Blessed Virgin's fiat.

Even though the Incarnation depended entirely upon God's precedent initiative, it nevertheless pleased him to make Its effecting contingent upon Mary's free consent. Such is also the case with the process by which the fruits of the redemption have been brought forth in the Christian era. Through the Sacraments God continuously extends those fruits through time, but for them to become manifest – both in man and, through him, in the world – it remains necessary for man to accept them.

The same synergistic principle is at work in the third fiat. Jesus wishes to see, in and through man, the consummation of God's work in creation and redemption. This is why he

---

[102] It is apparent that others who lived either at the same time Luisa did, or soon after, experienced a form of mystical union substantially similar to hers without having any awareness of her revelation. A book that summarizes this new movement of the Spirit is Hugh Owen's *New and Divine: The Holiness of the Third Christian Millennium* (Jacksonville: John Paul II Institute of Christian Spirituality, 2001).

extends to Luisa and, through her, to man, this new knowledge and invitation to live in the divine will. Whether it will actually happen, though, depends as it always has upon the fullness and the perfection of man's response.

Even from this perspective, though, a crucial question remains. How can it be said that the consummation of God's creative and redemptive works could depend upon events – i.e., Luisa Piccarreta's fiat and man's adherence to her private revelation – that are not explicitly prophesied by divine Revelation? The answer lies in the very fact that divine Revelation leaves open the question of how God will eventually consummate his works. We only know that he will do it; we do not know exactly how: "We do not know the time for the consummation of the earth and of humanity, nor do we know how all things will be transformed."[103]

In other words, while we cannot know with the certainty of faith that living in the divine will is necessary to bring about that consummation, neither can we know with the certainty of faith that it is *not* necessary. So, it is by the very fact of this uncertainty that the third fiat can be allowed for as a *possible* means, that is, so long as two criteria are satisfied.

First, because a third fiat and living in the divine will are not mentioned in divine Revelation as the means by which God will ultimately transform all things, we may not give such an idea the assent of religious faith. But so long as we do not assent to the idea with religious faith (and nothing in Luisa's writings says that we should) then we are free to assent to it with human faith. Cardinal Joseph Ratzinger restated this

---

[103] *Gaudium et Spes*, 39.

fundamental distinction between the assents of religious faith and human faith:

> The authority of private revelations is essentially different from that of the definitive public Revelation. The latter demands faith; in it in fact God himself speaks to us through human words and the mediation of the living community of the Church. Faith in God and in his word is different from any other human faith, trust or opinion. The certainty that it is God who is speaking gives me the assurance that I am in touch with truth itself. It gives me a certitude which is beyond verification by any human way of knowing. It is the certitude upon which I build my life and to which I entrust myself in dying. Private revelation is a help to this faith, and shows its credibility precisely by leading me back to the definitive public Revelation. In this regard, Cardinal Prospero Lambertini, the future Pope Benedict XIV, says in his classic treatise, which later became normative for beatifications and canonizations: "An assent of Catholic faith is not due to revelations approved in this way; it is not even possible. These revelations seek rather an assent of human faith in keeping with the requirements of prudence, which puts them before us as probable and credible to piety."[104]

Thus, we are free to assent with human faith to what Luisa's private revelation proposes if doing so would help us more

---

[104] From his "Theological Commentary In Preparation for the Release of the Third Part of the Secret of Fatima," *ibid.*

fully assent with religious faith to Christ's definitive Revelation, particularly his call to man to perfect himself and to transform the created order for and in God.

Second, we can give this assent of human faith to the propositions of Luisa's private revelation only if they do not contradict anything that *is* within the deposit of divine Revelation. This is especially important with respect to that limited set of revealed truths that describe how God will eventually consummate the works he has begun in and through man. What is that set of truths?

We know that a link has always existed between the destiny of man and the universe: "Revelation affirms the profound common destiny of the material world and man."[105] We further know that there is a causal relationship within that shared destiny, namely, man alone has free will and thus he alone bears the responsibility to fully respond to God and thereby fulfill not only his own destiny but the destiny of all creation. How was man to accomplish this?

We know only that his "work" from the beginning was to "collaborat(e)... with God in perfecting the visible creation."[106] Whatever that work was, by his original sin, he failed in it. By Christ's faithfulness, God in one sense completed this work for man, but in another sense he left it to be subsequently completed by, in and through man. In summary, we know only that God's creative and redemptive works will eventually be consummated, and that that

---

[105] CCC 1046.
[106] CCC 373.

consummation will be *somehow* linked to the fullness of man's response to God.

Luisa's private revelation expands upon these fundamental truths without contradicting any of them. Man's original collaborative work with God consisted of only one task: to live in the divine will. That is, man was to continuously co-operate with God in all that God does, thereby "giving voice" to God's love for man as it is manifested in every corner and moment of created existence. If man had only done this he would have accomplished his God-given assignment to perfect himself and all of creation. Moreover, this, his originally assigned work, not only remains to be completed, but until he completes it God's own work, first in creating and then in redeeming man and the universe, will remain "not yet completed." Christ won back for man the ability to live once again in the divine will and thereby accomplish his original "work." As man will live in this way again he will consummately perfect both himself and creation.

Thus, for the ultimate accomplishment of God's creative and redemptive works, what is alone "necessary," in the absolute sense of the word, is that man, in Christ, respond in the fullest way possible to all that God has done for him in Christ. It is not necessary, not in this same absolute sense anyway, that any particular person abide by or even know about Luisa's fiat and private revelation *per se*.

However, her writings could be considered as necessary in a certain relative sense, that is, if they happened to be the particular means by which a person came to better understand what God had originally asked of man, and how

God in Christ made it again possible for man to respond to that original, divine request. So, if it is true that some persons might arrive at the consummate and consummating mode of union with the divine will that Luisa describes without any exposure to her life or writings, it is also true that others might find her writings to be indispensable to arriving at it.

Distinguishing Luisa's fiat from Mary's.

The same distinctions that help us evaluate Luisa's unique, "necessary" role in effecting God's universal designs also help us evaluate those potentially problematic parallels that Jesus sometimes draws between her fiat and Mary's. Here are a few examples.

Jesus tells Luisa:

> My daughter, the First Fiat was said in Creation without the intervention of any creature. For completion of the Second Fiat I chose my Mother. Now for the completion of both I want to say the Third Fiat, which will complete the glory and honor of the Fiat of Creation, as well as will be the confirmation and development of the fruits of the Fiat of Redemption.[107]

> Just as in the Redemption I chose my incomparable Mother as a unifying link with Myself, from whom the fruits of the Redemption descended, so I chose you as a

---

[107] January 24, 1921, (12).

unifying link, from whom the Holiness of living in my Volition was to begin...[108]

Do you not want, then, that my Will descend upon earth? But just as Redemption had Its beginning in a Virgin - as I was not conceived in all men in order to redeem them, even though whoever wants it, can enter the good of Redemption and each one can receive Me in the Sacrament for himself alone – in the same way, now my Will must have Its beginning, possession, growth and development in one virgin creature. And then, whoever disposes himself and wants it, will enter the goods which the living in my Will contains. Had I not been conceived in my beloved Mama, Redemption would never have taken place. In the same way, if I do not operate the prodigy of making one soul live in my Supreme Will, the *'Fiat Voluntas Tua* on earth as it is in Heaven'*, will not take place in the human generations.[109]

Each of God's three fiats depends upon him first speaking his word. In the latter two, the subsequent effecting of his word depends upon the creature's response. But there is an essential difference that distinguishes those latter two interactions between the Creator's revelation and the creature's response.

All that God now "says" to man to and through Luisa he explicitly grounds in the fruits of the redemption, i.e., in everything that he already "said" to man by way of his definitive Revelation to and through Mary. In other words,

---

[108] December 3, 1921, (13).
[109] May 2, 1923, (15).

anything new that he might "say" to man through Luisa is not new in substance, but is a new explication of what he already "said" to man through Mary. He speaks his same word anew to Luisa, but now in such a way that man's same fundamental response to him might be dramatically amplified and indeed reach its perfection. Likewise, any new flowering of sanctity that might now "begin" as a result of man's heightened response to God would have its theological origin not in Luisa's fiat or her revelation, but in Mary's fiat and Christ's definitive Revelation.

So, beneath each of the parallels that Jesus sometimes draws between his respective revelations to Mary and Luisa and their respective responses there lies a difference of essence and not merely of degree. God's revelation to Mary and her fiat in response together formed the sole necessary means by which the Word became flesh. Her fiat was thus a unique and fundamentally unrepeatable event. All subsequent graces would flow from it.

In contrast, even if Luisa's fiat and writings could be said to release the greatest, heretofore undiscovered depth of graces, those graces would, like all graces, have their origin in the fountainhead of the redemption, that is, in Mary's fiat. Luisa is only to make better known by word and deed what Christ, through Mary, has already made definitively known by word and deed:

> As the Virgin was conceived in this seed exempt from every stain – what was all work of the Divine Fiat – Its Divine Kingdom was conceived again within humanity; and as the Immaculate little Virgin was born, the right to possess It was given back to

101

humanity. Now when I came upon earth to take on human flesh, I made use of the seed of the Sovereign Queen of Heaven, and it can be said that We worked together to form again this Kingdom of Ours in the human generations. There is nothing left but to know It in order to possess It.[110]

Indeed, my daughter, if no one had known that I had come upon earth, Redemption would have been something dead and without effects for creatures. So, knowledge gave life to Its fruits. The same will be for my Will: knowledge will give life to the fruits of my Will. This is why I wanted to renew what I did in Redemption, choosing another virgin, remaining hidden with her for forty years and more, segregating her from everyone as if in a new Nazareth, to be free with her of telling the whole story, the prodigies and the goods contained in It, so as to be able to form the life of my Will in you.[111]

Luisa's third fiat thus emerges as a "type" of Mary's second fiat. That is, Luisa's response to God is at once made possible by, and is entirely ordered toward the earthly fulfillment of, Mary's response to God. Likewise, Luisa's role as a "second virgin" – elsewhere also described as a "second link" – is only to more perfectly reveal and repeat the depths of the unique response of the *Virgo Singularis*: "You must be our echo, the echo of my Celestial Mamma, because it was She alone that lived perfectly and fully in the Supreme Will."[112]

---

[110] September 16, 1928, (24).
[111] June 15, 1926, (19).
[112] April 16, 1926, (19).

So, as arresting as the terms "second virgin" and "second link" might at first seem – perhaps more so to Luisa than to anyone else – the core sense in which Jesus uses them is fundamentally no different from the sense in which every Christian and the corporate Church is called to be a "second virgin" and a "second link" in the divine plan, that is, second after the original pattern of Mary.

In net effect, as Jesus elevates the new importance of Luisa and her fiat he does not thereby diminish the singularity and centrality of Mary and her fiat, but he in fact underscores them in a new way:

> It was really She (Mary) who received the seed of the 'Fiat Voluntas Tua,' as in Heaven so on earth, which ennobled and restored Her to the beginning – as it was when man was created by Us before he sinned. Indeed, She surpassed man and was embellished even more in the continuous flow of the Fiat that alone has the virtue of reproducing images similar to Him who created them.[113]

> So, around the Queen of Heaven many empty places can be seen, which can be occupied by no one else but Her copies. And since She was the first from the generation of my Will, the Kingdom of the Fiat will also be called "Kingdom of the Virgin."[114]

---

[113] December 8, 1923, (16).

[114] November 10, 1926, (20). That Mary's fiat is the source of living in the divine will and that she is the most perfect creaturely model of it is most evident in a book of meditations Luisa wrote entitled, "The Virgin Mary in the Kingdom of the Divine Will."

In summary, as significant as Jesus might portray Luisa's role and writings, and to whatever extent he might draw parallels between the necessity of her fiat and Mary's, he nevertheless insists, "No one can say that they have reached Us (Jesus and Mary) whether in suffering or in love. At the most they resemble Us in part; but to reach Us – no one."[115]

Likewise, Luisa's fiat at the most resembles Mary's fiat; it does not reach it. God desired Mary's fiat to be uniquely given, and forever viewed, within the same order as his definitive self-Revelation, and thereby to be forever associated with that sense in which his work was definitively "completed." In this regard, Luisa's fiat cannot be, should not be, and need not be compared with Mary's. This is because God desired Luisa's fiat, in contrast with Mary's, to be given, and forever viewed, within the order of private revelation, and thereby to be forever associated with that sense in which his work is "yet to be completed."

But so long as we keep in mind that fundamental distinction, then Luisa's fiat *can* be compared with Mary's, that is, as the echoed voice can be compared with the spoken original. While only the original can be considered necessary in the absolute sense, the echo *can be* considered necessary in a certain relative sense. That is, Luisa's echo might be "necessary" to the extent that it reveals an inner dimension of Mary's original that had not been perceived before. And as that inner dimension of Mary's fiat is newly heard it can be repeated, and as it is repeated it can be returned to God with her original, over and over again.

---

[115] August 22, 1926, (19).

Why this gift was not revealed at the time of the Incarnation: the fruit tree analogy

Jesus' revelations about living in the divine will make it clear that he did not want it to be considered in the same category as the many other spiritual developments that have taken place during the Christian era. Rather, it was to be understood as a unique, first manifestation of a previously unrealized dimension of God's definitive self-Revelation. Indeed the return of man to this original form of union with God was to be understood as the ultimate, core purpose of the Incarnation and redemption.

But if Jesus would have us believe that man living in the divine will is the ultimate fruit of his saving work, then why did he not reveal that fact during his earthly life? Moreover, does not his very claim to have held back this form of mystical union imply that Christianity is entering an essentially new order of salvation, a claim that would in effect put Luisa's spirituality out of continuity with Sacred Tradition?

It is not clear whether Luisa was aware of these theological concerns, but she did ask Jesus a number of times why, if he loves living in the divine will so much, he has waited almost two thousand years to make it known. Jesus explained that it was not that he did not want to manifest it earlier, but that mankind was not yet ready to receive it:

> I (Luisa) said: "My Love, if there is so much good in this living in the Divine Will, why didn't You manifest it before?" And He (Jesus): "My daughter, first I had to make known what my Humanity did

105

and suffered externally, to be able to dispose souls to knowing what my Divinity did inside. The creature is incapable of understanding my work all together; therefore I keep manifesting Myself little by little."[116]

Now, my daughter, when I came upon the earth, creatures were all illiterate about the things of Heaven; and, if I had wanted to speak about the Fiat and about living in it, they would have been incapable of understanding it. If they did not know the way to come to Me, it was because they were, for the greater part, lame, blind, sick; and I had to abase myself to the strippings of my Humanity which covered that Fiat that I wanted to give, in order to fraternize with them, to associate myself with everyone, so to be able to teach the first rudiments, the a,b,c's of the Supreme Fiat. And all that I taught, did and suffered was not other than to prepare the way, the Kingdom and the dominion of my Will.[117]

He sometimes used the analogy of a tree that can bear its fruit, i.e., manifest its ultimate inner purpose, only when it has reached its season of maturity:

My daughter, the primary purpose of my coming upon the earth was really that man would return into the bosom of my Volition as he went forth when he was created. To do that, though, my Volition had to form, by means of my Humanity, the roots, the trunk,

---

[116] January 29, 1919, (12).
[117] March 28, 1926, (19).

the branches, the leaves, the blossoms from which must come forth the Celestial fruits of my Volition.[118]

This is the image of my Church. The seed is my Will, in which She was born and raised. But in order for the tree to grow, it takes time; and in order for some trees to give fruit, it takes the length of centuries - the more precious the plant is, the longer it takes. The same for the tree of my Will, which is the most precious, the most noble and divine, the highest, and therefore it took time for it to grow, and for its fruits to be made known. So, the Church has known the seed, and there is no sanctity without it; then She has known the branches, but it is always the same tree that She has been around. Now She must know the fruits in order to nourish Herself and to enjoy them; and this will be all my glory and my crown, as well as of all virtues and of the entire Church. Now, what is your wonder, if instead of manifesting the fruits of my Will before, I have manifested them to you after so many centuries? If the tree was not yet formed, how could I make the fruits known?[119]

The developing tree analogy - a classic for the organically developing doctrines of the Church - offers a sense in which the release of the gift of living in the divine will could have been delayed until now. But it also helps explain several other issues about living in the divine will. 1. It shows that this spirituality is organically dependent upon prior forms of sanctity. 2. It shows how this spirituality can be seen

---

[118] January 28, 1926. (18).
[119] November 28, 1922, (15).

simultaneously as both novel to, and continuous with, the spiritual tradition that has preceded it. 3. It offers a sense in which this spirituality can belong to a new and higher order than the forms that have preceded it. 4. It offers a sense in which this spirituality could have been withheld from prior generations. 5. It helps explain the claim that until now man had not yet been ready for this gift. Let us examine each of these issues.

1. Divine will spirituality is organically connected to and dependent upon the Church's spiritual tradition.

The fruit tree analogy demonstrates that this newly emerging spiritual gift must not be viewed as a form of holiness that devalues or circumvents prior forms. On contrary, it can only emerge from an organic foundation of their prior attainment, just like fruit can only emerge from the blossoms of a mature tree. Jesus insists that as a prerequisite to entering into this mode of union with him, "one must first practice the lesser forms of holiness, which are like a retinue, forerunners, messengers, and preparations for this Holiness that is completely Divine."[120]

Furthermore, the way of the cross that has always been essential to growth in Christian holiness (the sap of the tree, so to speak) continues to be essential to this new fruit: "Thus the pains, the mortifications, the vigilance, the patience and even my privations will serve to enlarge and guard the boundaries of my Will in your soul."[121] So, to live in the

---

[120] December 3, 1921, (13).
[121] August 28, 1923, (16).

divine will, spiritual maturity and persistence are presupposed.

2. *Divine will spirituality is both novel to and in continuity with the Church's spiritual tradition.*

The analogy shows how living in the divine will can be both novel to the Apostolic Tradition and continuous with It. Before the fruit is seen upon the tree for the first time, it is, in a sense, "unknown" to the tree. But we do not immediately reject it when it first appears, for we must consider whether the potential for it has always been there, even when the tree was only a seed. And so we test it to ensure that what might appear to be a newly emerging, endogenous fruit is not, in fact, an exogenous parasite in disguise.

For example, as mistletoe appears and develops on a tree it might seem beautiful, but upon testing it we discover that its life is not organically continuous with the life of the tree. Unlike fruit, its organic origin does not reach back to the tree as a seed. Rather, its organic origin is at the point where it attaches to the tree. But, to the point, the test for the organic origin of this newly emerging life form is not merely in determining whether it exactly replicates a precedent form of the tree's life.

Likewise, living in the divine will must be tested for doctrinal continuity. We must ensure that this new form of mystical union has its organic origin not in Luisa's private revelation but in Christ's definitive Revelation. In other words, does it blossom forth from the same continuous Christian vision that has preceded it, or is it essentially exterior to that vision?

But, as with the analogy to the tree and its first fruit, we cannot adequately answer this question merely by determining that this new form does not exactly replicate some form that has preceded it.[122] Rather, we must go to a deeper question: Do the essential principles of this new form correspond to the essential datum of divine Revelation? If so, then living in the divine will can be considered organically continuous with the Apostolic Tradition even if no apostle or saint had ever articulated it or experienced it exactly as such.

3. Living in the divine will is a new form of holiness but not a new era of holiness.

To say that the new, fruit-bearing phase of the tree's life manifests its ultimate, previously hidden purpose is not to suggest that the tree is thereby beginning an essentially new life. Likewise, for Luisa's writings to claim that living in the divine will brings forth the ultimate, previously hidden purpose of the redemption is not to suggest that the era of salvation is giving way to an essentially new era. Rather, it is to distinguish, within the same organically continuous era, an extraordinary moment of metamorphosis from the process of ordinary, linear growth that has preceded it.

In one sense, the two phases are no different. The emergence of a new leaf belongs to the same fundamental order as the emergence of a new fruit, because each event depends and

---

[122] Some might disagree, insisting in effect that every possible manifestation of the gift of mystical union has been continuously, fully present in the Church in at least one person from the first moment of her existence. I respond to this objection in the following section, "Respecting the sanctity of the saints."

expands upon the same inner life principle of the tree. But in another sense, they are essentially different events. The emergence of a new fruit belongs to a higher order than the emergence of a new leaf because it singularly reveals the ultimate, innermost purpose of the tree.

Likewise, living in the divine will belongs to the same fundamental order as all the other developments of the era of salvation. It is nourished by the same sacramental life and it reaches out toward the same fundamental objectives, i.e., the salvation and sanctification of man and the restoration of the created order. But it also belongs to a different and higher order because it singularly discloses the ultimate, innermost purposes of creation and redemption, that is, for God and man each to fully "co-operate" as one in all that the other does. This is the consummate manner in which man restores all things in Christ, so that God might be all and in all.[123]

Another way in which living in the divine will could be said to singularly embody the core purposes of creation and redemption is in how it interconnects the fulfillment of man's earthly destiny with a return to his origin.[124] It is akin to how the fruit singularly embodies both the tree's origin, that is, its seed, and its destiny, that is, its flesh of nourishment.

---

[123] C.f. I Cor. 15:28.

[124] The dominance of this theme is summarized in the title Jesus gave Luisa for her diary: *Book of Heaven: The Recall of the Creature to the Order, to the Place, and to the Purpose for which it was created by God.*

On the one hand this interconnection is certainly not new to the Christian Tradition. Through baptism into Christ's death and resurrection, man is retrospectively restored to all the dignity of his original relationship with God, while he is prospectively given an earthly foretaste of his ultimate heavenly destiny. Furthermore, as he journeys toward Christian maturity, he grows into the image of the One who is both the origin and the destiny of his faith: "I live, no longer I, but Christ lives in me."[125] It is the well-worn path of the saints.

And yet Luisa's writings take this same principle of man's interconnected origin and destiny and open it to a new and vastly expanded dimension. Our baptismal return to the pristine state of Adam and Eve not only restores us to the original dignity they lost at the fall, it also empowers us to pick up their collaborative work with God where they left off.

That is, united to the soul of Christ's humanity, we are enabled to join with him in diffusing all of man's finite actions into the eternal reaches of Christ's divinity, thereby returning to the Father all the glory and praise that has been his due from the creature since the dawn of time. This finally accomplishes, in and through man, God's original plan for creation and redemption. And as we retrospectively, consummately image him who is our origin, so does he give us a prospective, consummate foretaste on earth of our destiny with him in heaven. Jesus describes this experience as the fulfillment of a prayer he gave us during his earthly life:

---

[125] Gal. 2:20.

Then, I (Luisa) was thinking to myself: "In the 'Our Father', Our Lord teaches us to say - to pray: 'Your Will be done'. Now, why does He say that He wants us to live in It?" And Jesus, always benign, moving in my interior, told me: "My daughter, 'your Will be done' which I taught in the 'Our Father' meant that all were to pray that they might at least do the Will of God. And this is for all Christians and for all times; nor can anyone call himself a Christian if he does not dispose himself to do the Will of his Celestial Father. But you have not thought of the other addition which comes immediately after: 'On earth as It is in Heaven'. 'On earth as It is in Heaven' means to live in the Divine Will; it means to pray that the Kingdom of my Will may come on earth in order to live in It. In Heaven, they not only do my Will, but they live in It – they possess It as their own thing, and as their own Kingdom. And if they did It, but did not possess It, their happiness would not be full, because true happiness begins in the depth of the soul. To do the Will of God does not mean to possess It, but to submit oneself to Its commands, while to live in It is possession. Therefore, in the 'Our Father', in the words 'your Will be done' is the prayer that all may do the Supreme Will, and in 'on earth as It is in Heaven', that man may return into that Will from which he came, in order to reacquire his happiness, the lost goods, and the possession of his Divine Kingdom."[126]

---

[126] October 15, 1926, (20). St. Annibale di Francia offered these comments in his General Preface to Luisa's writings: "The third *Fiat* was left to us by Our Lord Jesus Christ in the great Prayer of the Our Father, with

4. How divine will spirituality can be said to have been held back from man until now.

When Jesus tells Luisa that the gift of living in the divine will has been until now "held back" from man, it is in the sense of a fruit of the redemption having been held *within* the life of the Church. It is not in the sense of a graft or a supplement to the redemption that he has withheld from the Church from *without*. Jesus says that the greater part of what he gained for man through his hidden life and the hidden pains of his passion, and which he subsequently entrusted to the Church, remains yet to be released:

> The complete fruit has not been taken by creatures. I await those who must live in my Volition so that they will no longer be suspended but poured out, releasing their complete fruit upon creatures for their good. Only those who must live in my Will will liberate my goods from this suspension.[127]

These fruits of the redemption remain suspended most especially in the Sacraments, and living in the divine will is explicitly ordered toward releasing them: "See then, how the Sacrament of the Eucharist - and not only that one, but all the Sacraments, left to my Church and instituted by Me - will give all the fruits which they contain and complete

---

those divine words: *'Fiat Voluntas Tua Sicut in Coelo et in terra'* – Thy Will be done on earth as it is in Heaven. This supplication of the third *Fiat* which has resounded for twenty centuries on the lips of the children of the Holy Church, in the Royal Priesthood of the great Sacrifice of Holy Mass – this supplication, in spite of all the human oppositions and iniquities, must have its great fulfillment. It cannot remain unanswered."
[127] October 4, 1925, (18).

fulfillment, when Our bread - the Will of God - is done on earth as it is in Heaven."[128]

Yes, heaven and earth are full of God's glory, but how much of that glory yet waits to be released by, in and through man?

5. A spirituality that man was not yet ready for.

Finally, the tree and fruit analogy helps to explain how until now man has been "not yet ready" to receive the gift of living in the divine will. When the young tree first emerges from the ground, it is not yet ready to bear even one fruit, let alone its full harvest. It must first develop a sufficiently strong structure of roots, trunk and branches, and that process might take several years. In the same sense Jesus told Luisa that the Kingdom of the Redemption first needed to expand, strengthen and mature before it could finally bear its fruit in the Kingdom of his Will.

Divine Revelation does in fact allow and even predict that subsequently unfolding depths of truth will become manifest according to the Church's ever-growing strength. Jesus said in his farewell discourse, "I have yet many things to say to you, but you cannot bear them now. When the Spirit of truth comes, he will guide you into all the truth."[129]

Jesus did not mean that he was withholding from the Church anything essential to man's salvation and sanctification. Rather, he meant that though God had

---

[128] May 2, 1923, (15).
[129] John 16:12-13.

115

definitively revealed himself to man in the Word made flesh, yet some dimensions of his self-Revelation would have to be disclosed later as the developing Church grew in her ability to assimilate and transmit to man what God had revealed in Christ.

In his comments on this passage from John's Gospel, Cardinal Joseph Ratzinger describes an historical process in which the Spirit gradually discloses knowledge that becomes reachable only as the Church's foundational body of premises grows:

> On the one hand, the Spirit acts as a guide who discloses a knowledge previously unreachable because the premise was missing -- this is the boundless breadth and depth of Christian faith. On the other hand, to be guided by the Spirit is also "to draw from" the riches of Jesus Christ himself, the inexhaustible depths of which appear in the way the Spirit leads.[130]

Any new depth of knowledge the Spirit discloses to the maturing Church is necessarily ordered toward a new depth of love. I repeat a point made earlier: This principle need not imply that the Church's ever-expanding deposit of objective knowledge sets the ever-expanding outer limit to her capacity to love. But it could imply that some dimensions of God's revealed love for man (and, by implication, man's love for God and for his fellow man)

---

[130] *Ibid*, "Theological Commentary In Preparation for the Release of the Third Part of the Secret of Fatima."

might not have been as well appreciated by – and reflected in – the early Church as they are in the modern Church.

For instance, the primitive Church was perhaps "not yet ready to bear" all that the Spirit would later say to the modern Church about such matters as the nature of Mary's role in the plan of redemption, religious liberty, ecumenism, and capital punishment. So, as the Church's knowledge has grown, so has she become more able to bear – that is, to support and to transmit to man – the plenitude of God's love for man revealed in Christ.

This then is what Jesus means about having waited until now to make known the gift of living in the divine will. As centrally important to him as it is, man – in and through his medium to God, which is the Church – was in earlier years not yet capable of bearing it.[131]

Respecting the sanctity of the saints.

What does it say about the saints of the first nineteen Christian centuries if we say that living in the divine will is the consummate fruit of the redemption only now becoming fully manifest? Does it mean that they did not live in the divine will? Does it call into question the thoroughness of

---

[131] I recognize that this explanation leaves unanswered the question of how exactly it is that the Church, which was not able to bear the gift of living in the divine will in earlier centuries, has now become able. What developments have made it possible? Luisa's original literature offers no conclusive answers. Jesus only claims the fact generally, he does not explain it specifically. But perhaps this was with good reason, for a mystical encounter would not seem to be the venue for an exploration in the history of theology.

God's generous love for these saints? Does it imply that they were less than fully generous in their response to him?

I offer a threefold reply to these questions. First, the fact that God is generous to all does not necessarily mean that he distributes his spiritual gifts in equal measure. Second, the experience of living in the divine will was, in fact, not entirely unknown to the saints. Luisa's experience may have been greater than theirs, but it was nevertheless in fundamental continuity with theirs. Third, because of the manner in which Luisa's writings sometimes contrast living in the divine will with not living in it, some caution is indeed necessary to ensure that the lives of the saints are viewed as nonetheless exemplary.

1. The generosity of God and his saints.

Might God have withheld the gift of living in the divine will from earlier generations of saints? Scripture and Tradition offer no clear and certain answer. It is true that Christians of all generations have been assured of the unreserved nature of God's generous love made manifest in Christ Jesus. "(I)n him you were enriched in every way... so that you are not lacking in any spiritual gift as you wait for the revelation of our Lord Jesus Christ."[132] "Blessed be the God and Father of our Lord Jesus Christ, who has blessed us in Christ with every spiritual blessing in the heavens."[133]

Such assurances might seem to imply that even if living in the divine will has not been explicitly catalogued, in either

---

[132] I Cor. 1:5-7.
[133] Eph. 1:3.

Scripture or the testimonies of the saints, with the various spiritual gifts, we nevertheless could, and perhaps should, conclude that it has been continuously present in every phase of Christian history. But such an interpretation would have to be qualified.

While it is true that God always gives himself fully to all, it is also true that he does not necessarily give himself equally to all. This distinction is obvious among individual Christians. Though "all are called to sanctity and have received an equal privilege of faith,"[134] God does not make all of his spiritual gifts equally manifest in every believer: "There are different kinds of spiritual gifts but the same Spirit; there are different forms of service but the same Lord; there are different workings but the same God who produces all of them in everyone."[135]

Indeed he might choose one to manifest a greater and fuller share of those gifts than another, perhaps even in a manner that might seem unfair and unreasonable to us. But even in his doing so we should not conclude that he ever gives himself more fully to one than to another.

The same principle could be said to apply across the life span of an individual Christian. Certain spiritual gifts that might not be as fully apparent and utilized in one stage of his life can become so in another. But this does not mean that God had loved him the less during those periods in which any particular gift had been "withheld."

---

[134] *Lumen Gentium*, 32.
[135] I Cor. 12:4-6 ff.

Would not the same logic apply to the various phases of the Church's life? While the Church is holy and beloved of God in every age, this does not preclude the Spirit from making certain spiritual gifts more fully manifest in one age than in another. Perhaps this is why Sacred Scripture and Tradition do not set any one saint or any one age of the Church, including any apostle or the apostolic age, as the definitive outer limit and measure of Christian sanctity.[136]

Indeed, the apostles themselves knew that the power of Christ at work within the newly conceived Church contained a transforming potential that far exceeded even what they could imagine based upon their own extraordinary experiences.[137]

Thus, through the centuries the Church continuously transmits to each new generation the same essential power by which man is made holy, but without ever limiting the form and measure of the spiritual gifts to that which has been made manifest in earlier generations.

In short, nothing in divine Revelation precludes the possibility that the Lord could bestow upon, i.e., draw forth from within, the same, continuous life of the Church a new

---

[136]Even Pope Leo XIII in his exaltation of St. Joseph in *Quamquam Pluries* does not do this. Leo writes, "it may not be doubted that (St. Joseph) approached nearer than any to the eminent dignity by which the Mother of God surpasses so nobly all created natures." But "dignity" here refers only to the surpassing rank of St. Joseph's office as the spouse of Mary and the putative father of Jesus. It is not also a commentary upon his holiness. While his rank and his holiness are no doubt intertwined, they are nevertheless distinguishable.
[137] Eph. 3:20.

form of the gift of mystical union that had not been manifested earlier. It is even possible that that new manifestation could express and accomplish the core purposes of the redemption in a way that nothing before it ever had. To propose as much is not to call into question the continuity and totality of God's generous love for his Church and his saints.

The same is true as we view the matter from the perspective of the saints. Because it is ultimately God and not man who decides which person will receive what spiritual gift and when he or she will receive it, nothing negative is implied about the generosity of any saint who does not receive a particular gift that God freely chooses to give to another. Certainly, growth in the spiritual life depends upon a synergism between God and man, and man no doubt must play his part. To develop the spiritual gifts given to us at baptism we must persist in our sincere desires and efforts to love God.

But our role is only one side of this dramatic dialogue. God also plays his role, and it is the principal one. Thus, we grow in the spiritual life not only according to our initiatives, but also and even more crucially according to the Lord's initiatives.

So, yes, he calls each and all to the heights of holiness, and, yes, to arrive there we must do everything we humanly can – of course, even then, only because we are aided by grace – to make the ascent. But the gifts we ultimately receive at the summit of the spiritual life, i.e., the gifts of mystical union, we receive only as God wills it. They are not dispensed according to our human desires, no matter how pure. They are not produced by our human efforts, no matter how earnest. This is why St. Teresa of Avila describes infused contemplation as a gift that God gives entirely according to his own designs: "...the Lord gives when He desires and as He desires and to whom He desires. Since these blessings belong to Him, He does no injustice to anyone."[138]

Because these gifts of spiritual union are ultimately given according to God's prerogatives and not man's, I would have no reason either to boast or to complain if I were to compare what he has given me with what he has given others. Likewise, I would have no reason either to be proud or dismayed if I were to look back over my life in Christ and consider what gifts might have been more operative at which phases. My only occupation should be to remain faithful to God in the present moment. It is not to be preoccupied about what gifts I have received (or not received) from him, or when and in what measure I have received them.

Again, is it not reasonable that the same principle would also apply over the life span of the Church? Is it not true that she too would change, adapt and grow in the various forms, expressions and experiences of the spiritual gifts? Furthermore, as it is true for the individual Christian so it is true for the Church: these developments occur only according to a fundamental synergy that involves both her and the Spirit. On her part, the Church must persist in her sincere desires and efforts. But it is ultimately the Spirit, working according to God's own hidden designs, who unfolds in her what he wills, and when he wills it.

---

[138] *The Interior Castle*, Mansion 4, Chapter 1.

So, to say that he might only now be bestowing upon the Church the full measure of the gift of living in the divine will would not be to say anything disparaging about the Church's continuous holiness and fidelity to the Lord. Likewise, it would not imply that any saint of any previous century did not live a life of authentic and exemplary holiness. No, they fully received and they fully gave in the manner and to the measure to which God had uniquely called them.

2. Seeing the gift of living in the divine will in continuity with the lives of the saints.

If it is true in one sense that living in the divine will is a new gift given to the Church now, it is also true in another sense that it is a gift that has already and always belonged to the Church and her saints in the past. Jesus obliquely affirmed this fact to Luisa. On one occasion she marveled at "the goodness of Our Lord in sharing all His goods with me, without excluding me from anything of all that He contained." Jesus replied,

> Dear daughter of Mine, don't be surprised at what you are seeing because you are not alone or unique. During all times I kept souls and made them able to receive, to the extent to which a creature can perfectly receive, the purpose of My Creation, Redemption and Sanctification. I made sure that the creature would be able to contain all the blessings for which I created, redeemed and sanctified it; otherwise, if I had not done so -- at all times, even with one single person -- all My work would be thwarted, at least for a time. This is the order of My Providence, My Justice and of My Love; that is, that in every era there would be at

least one soul to whom I can give and share all the blessings, all the goods in store for it, and that the creature would give Me all it owed Me as a creature.[139]

So, while Jesus on the one hand describes the gift of living in the divine will as "new" and Luisa as the "first" to receive it, on the other hand he points out within it a thread of continuity that reaches back through every age of the Church. God has been continuously disposed to give it, while the Church and her saints have been continuously disposed to receive it.

Likewise, if the process by which this gift is now becoming fully manifest can be fairly characterized as a movement from potency to actualization or from the implicit to the explicit, this is not to say that in earlier years it had been entirely dormant. It is, rather, to say that earlier generations of Christian saints might not have grasped it as fully, or utilized it as maximally. But it has nevertheless always been "active" within the Church, at least in some inchoate sense. Here is an illustration.

Luisa's revelation characterizes living in the divine will as the ultimate, implicitly longed-for fulfillment of the Lord's Prayer petition that the will of the Father be done "on earth as it is heaven." But this need not imply that before her revelation Christians were not already, in some true sense, living that same reality. Indeed, the Church has always believed that even now here on earth we are already living the same substantial life that the blessed live in heaven.

---

[139] September 4, 1905, (6).

As Cardinal Ratzinger describes it, "eternal life" is not a reality that we only await in the future, but it is one that we already live in this present moment. "Present and eternity are not, like present and future, located side by side and separated; rather, they are interwoven." Likewise, that petition of the Lord's Prayer does not only prophesy a state that will be fulfilled in man at some later date. It also describes a reality that the baptized are already living here and now. The Cardinal explains,

> (E)ternal life becomes effective in the midst of time. For that means that God's will is done "on earth, as it is in heaven." Earth becomes heaven, becomes the Kingdom of God, whenever God's will is done there as in heaven. We pray for this because we know that it does not lie within our power to draw heaven down here. For the Kingdom of God is *his* Kingdom, not our kingdom, not within our sway; because it is so, it is final and can be relied upon. But it is always quite near wherever God's will is accepted... The Kingdom of God is... not a chronological future, does not come chronologically later, but refers at all times to the wholly other, which for that very reason is able to embed itself within time, so as simply to take it up within itself and make of it pure presence. Eternal life, which takes its beginning in communion with God here and now, seizes this here and now and takes it up within the great expanse of true reality, which is no longer fragmented by the stream of time. There the mutual impermeability of I and thou can no longer exist, as this is closely associated with the fragmentation of time. In fact, anyone who sets his will within the will of God deposits it right there,

where all good will has its place; and thus our will blends with the will of all others. Wherever this happens, the saying becomes true: I live, and yet no longer I – Christ lives in me.[140]

And if it is true that in every age of the Church Christians have known, at least in some nascent sense, the reality of doing the Father's will "on earth as it is in heaven," it is all the more true that the saints have known it even more fully. But this does not necessarily mean that they knew it with the clearest possible awareness. Nor does it necessarily mean that they employed that knowledge with the fullest possible intent, and thus to its greatest possible efficacy.

Which saint, for instance, has shown as intricately as Luisa has, that continuously doing the divine will in this eternal manner represents the original state of man's union with God? Which saint has so systematically explained its reparative potential? Which has so purposefully linked its determined practices to the ultimate consummation of man's destiny in Christ?

The dynamic of the third fiat then is not so much a matter of God finally giving the Church the gift of living in the divine will as if that gift were something entirely new to her. No,

---

[140] Cardinal Joseph Ratzinger, "My Joy is to be in Thy Presence: On the Christian Belief in Eternal Life," in *God is Near Us: The Eucharist, the Heart of Life*, (San Francisco: Ignatius Press, 2003), pp. 141, 143. This was originally a lecture given to the Christian Academy in Prague, March 30, 1992. It was published under the title: "Dass Gott Alles in Allem sei, Vom christlichen Glauben an das ewige Legen" ["That God may be all in all": Concerning the Christian belief in eternal life], in *Klerusblatt* 72 (1992): 203-7.

the Church has always known the gift of the indwelling, eternal divine will, and it has been made especially evident in the lives of her saints.

Rather, the third fiat is a matter of God helping the Church understand and utilize this gift far more profoundly. Thus, "the gift" is not a new dispensation of divine love, but a new appreciation and appropriation of the very same love that God has already dispensed through creation and redemption. Jesus tells Luisa,

> To the degree that (a man) recognizes the value of his gem he becomes richer and has a greater love and esteem for the gem. He treats it with more jealous care, knowing that it is his entire fortune, whereas before, he had treated it as though it were nothing And yet, the gem has not changed from what it was. The change has taken place in the man with his better understanding of the true value of the gem.[141]

So, to do God's will "on earth as it is in heaven" in the manner that Jesus describes to Luisa does not mean relating to God in a mode that has been entirely unknown to previous generations of Christian saints. Rather, it means more radically and purposefully seizing upon and utilizing the very same, eternal reality that has been continuously active within the Church for two thousand years, especially in the lives of her saints.

---

[141] August 25, 1921. (13).

3. Maintaining a due respect for the saints.

Because Luisa's writings characterize the sanctity of living in the divine will as far surpassing the sanctity of the saints, it is important that this not be taken as a slight against them. This point is clear enough on those occasions when Luisa, with specific reference to the saints, asks Jesus how this new gift could differ from or add to their already exalted experiences. He would explain, for example:

> No one else has entered into my Divine Will to do everything that my Humanity did. My Saints have done my Will, but they have not entered within to take part in all that my Will does and to take as within a blink of the eye all acts from the first to the last man and make themselves actors, spectators, and divinizers.[142]

> Search through the lives of as many Saints as you wish or in all the books of doctrine, and you will not find the prodigies of my Will operating in the creature and the creature operating in mine. At most you will find resignation, abandonment and union of wills, but not my Divine Will operating in the creature and the creature, in turn, operating in the Divine Will. This means that the time had not arrived in which my Goodness should call the creature to live in this sublime state.[143]

---

[142] January 24, 1923, (15).
[143] October 6, 1922, (14).

So, even as Jesus explains that what he is giving the Church now is a greater measure than what he gave the saints earlier, he wants us to know that what he gave them was nevertheless great and exemplary. In other words, he would have us continue to view them as entirely pleasing to him.

In other passages, however, this essential point is not so clearly made. For instance, Jesus often compares living in the divine will with not living in it, and in many of these comparisons the latter state is portrayed as less than pleasing to God. It is true that these comparisons do not *explicitly* refer to the saints. But given the fact that living in the divine will is on other occasions compared against the sanctity of the saints, might these negative comparisons *implicitly* refer to the saints? Jesus says this, for example:

> My daughter, how the creature goes to the bottom when he does not live in Our Will! He may do good; but, since the light of Our Will and the strength of Our holiness are missing, the good he does is covered with smoke. It blinds him from seeing and it produces egotism, vainglory, a self-love that becomes poisonous. Thus the creature cannot produce anything really good, either for himself or for others. Good works – how poor they are without My Will! ... At most they result in self-satisfaction... And oh, you can tell right away the person who does not live in It: He wants to do one thing today, tomorrow another; he wants to make a sacrifice at one time, another time he runs away from it. You can't rely on that person.

He is like a reed that moves when the wind of his passions start to blow.[144]

So, the soul in whom my will does not reign puffs out darkness, shadow and restlessness, and if she does any good, it is a good invested with fog. Her air is always unhealthy, her fruits unripe, her beauty faded.[145]

Certainly Jesus is not referring to the lives of the saints here, is he? Indeed, in light of what the saints have written about the life of mystical union,[146] these particular contrasts would seem to prove that they *did* live in the divine will.

How then are we to understand such disparaging descriptions? In Luisa's literature it seems that there are two senses in which "living in the divine will" is contrasted against other forms of union between the divine and human wills.

---

[144] April 26, 1938, (36).

[145] July 23, 1928 (24).

[146] For instance, in his manual on the writings of the Carmelite masters, *Fire Within* (San Francisco: Ignatius, 1989), p. 183, Fr. Thomas Dubay, S.M. summarizes well the interior life of one who has reached the summit of the spiritual life: "In the transforming union one is so closely bonded to God that all of this person's first inclinations are directed to the Lord Who originates them. In memory, intellect, will and desire there is no movement contrary to the divine will and goodness. From the first instant and without intellectual advertence, one's spontaneous movements are toward patience in adversity, thanksgiving and praise in prosperity, temperance in delightful occupations, love and chastity in human relations, toward God in everything. One does not even 'experience the first motions of sin.'"

In the first sense, "living in the divine will" is used to describe the general state of a Christian soul who lives in intimate union with God's will, whether it be Luisa or any other saintly person. Jesus favorably compares this exalted state with the unfortunately far more common state in which a Christian soul seeks only to obey God's will and nothing more. While this latter state is certainly commendable when contrasted with a complete disregard for God's will, it is not the terminus of Christian perfection. The soul has not yet freed himself from attachments to self-interest and self-satisfaction. He is not stable in his dispositions. For him the spiritual life is mostly a matter of principles of duty to God that are fulfilled from a safe distance away from God. He is thus not yet entirely pleasing to God. By contrasting living in the divine will with this inferior state of union, Jesus does not mean to relegate the saints to that latter state. Rather, he calls all souls who are content to linger in it to move onward – as the saints did – to the higher realms of intimate union with him.

In the second sense, Jesus contrasts the new experience of mystical union that he is revealing to and through Luisa with previous experiences of mystical union. These comparisons are, so to speak, between "living in the divine will" in the very specific, Luisan sense, with "living in the divine will" in the more general, classic sense. Every soul who has experienced the state of mystical union could testify with Luisa that his will has, in some sense, been mystically annihilated into the divine will. He no longer merely does the divine will, but in a sense he "lives in the divine will." He has become entirely passively disposed to receive from Jesus whatever he might wish to give, and do whatever Jesus might ask: "The behavior of living solely for God was practiced by the Saints."[147] All souls who have reached this state are entirely pleasing to God. The point Jesus makes in these comparisons, though, is that even within this exalted, exemplary state there can be, according to God's will, gradations.[148]

Thus, in one sense the saints could be said to have not lived in the divine will, that is, in the specific sense that God did not call them to live in it to the degree that Luisa did. But their lives remain nonetheless exemplary, because in the other, more general sense they did live in the divine will, that is, inasmuch as they went beyond merely doing God's will and lived in the realms of intimate union with his will.

Concluding thoughts on the saints

Even if it might be theoretically possible for there to be a form of mystical union – and an associated form of holiness – higher than the saints', how is such a notion conceivable in light of the already supremely exalted, sublime accounts they have given us? Does it not implicitly insult them even to try to conceive of a higher form of union?

---

[147] February 28, 1912, (11).

[148] The saints would not disagree. For instance, while St. John of the Cross affirms that mystical union is "the most that God communicates to the soul at this time (i.e., in this life)," he does not mean to say that every potential within this exalted state has been fully realized in every saint of every generation. He explains: "Yet it must not be thought that He communicates to all those who reach this state everything... or that He does so in the same manner and measure of knowledge and feeling. To some souls He gives more and to others less, to some in one way and to others in another, although all alike may be in this same state of spiritual espousal." *The Spiritual Canticle*, Stanzas 14 and 15, paragraph 2.

First, to the question of whether a higher form of union is even conceivable, we must keep in mind that holiness has both seen and unseen dimensions. Heroic virtue – human and theological – is the measure of holiness as we can see it in this life. And in this concrete, palpable dimension it would indeed be impossible to conceive of a greater holiness than that of the saints.

But in the dimension that we cannot see – the eternal dimension seen only by God – it is a different matter. The measure of holiness there is the extent to which God gratuitously lifts the creature into the reaches of his own uncreated, eternal kenosis. We can allow for the possibility of higher and lower forms of holiness in this unseen dimension not because we are able to conceptualize and measure them, but precisely because we are not able to.

Consider what this might mean for the gift of living in the divine will. Clearly it does not differ from the sanctity of the saints at the level of what can be observed and measured. To live in the divine will we must live lives of heroic virtue with no less determination than they did. In fact, if we are not continuously pursuing holiness at this basic, concrete level, we can be quite sure that we are not really pursuing it at the more sublime, eternal level either. But assuming that we are genuinely pursuing union with God within this realm that we can see with our natural eyes, Luisa's writings can open up vast, new possibilities of union with him within that realm that we can see only with the eyes of faith:

> So the soul, operating in the light of my Volition, unites itself to that single act of its Creator; and its operation takes place in the surroundings of the Light

of Eternity. Therefore, you cannot see your acts, nor in which part of the Light you have done them, nor where they are, because, for the creature, the Eternal Light of God is impassable and not able to be fully crossed; but it certainly knows that its act is there in the Light and that it takes place in the past, in the present, and in the future.[149]

In doing her act, the creature makes it small and limited, but as it enters into my Will, it becomes immense, it invests all, it gives light and heat to all, it reigns over all, it acquires supremacy over all the other acts of creatures - it has right over all. Therefore, she rules, she dominates, she conquers; yet, her act is small, but by doing it in my Will, it went through an incredible transformation, which not even Angels are allowed to comprehend. I alone can measure the just value of these acts done in my Will.[150]

So, while the observable human act remains essentially the same, its accompanying disposition and intention are elevated dramatically. This in turn exponentially multiplies the unseen efficacy of the act. Thus, by God's sheer, gratuitous gift, a consequent, extraordinary growth takes place in the person's sanctity: "(Jesus:) Their sanctity (those who will live in the divine will) will be so high that, like suns, they will eclipse the most beautiful stars of the saints of the past generations."[151] But, paradoxically, this growth must follow along the very same, self-forgetful trajectory of

---

[149] December 25, 1925, (18).
[150] December 12, 1917, (12).
[151] November 20, 1917, (12).

the saints, namely, it must be a movement *beyond* any unseemly concerns about one's own sanctity:

> Jesus: "Whoever thinks only of sanctifying herself, lives at the expense of her own sanctity, of her own strength, of her own love. Oh, how she will grow miserable!"[152]

> Luisa: "(My 'yes') was a 'yes' that had the seal and power of the Divine Volition, not pronounced for fear, or for personal interest of sanctity but only for living in the Volition of Jesus and for running for the good of all, as well as for giving Jesus Divine glory, love, and reparations."[153]

In the final analysis, we must remember that greatness in the realm of sanctity is measured according to the inverted logic of the Gospel: "Whoever wishes to be great among you will be your servant; whoever wishes to be first among you will be the slave of all."[154] So, a greater sanctity than the sanctity of the saints is conceivable because it is conceivable that God could gratuitously show us, on the unseen horizons of eternity, a way to outdo them in that happy contest of mutual, self-emptying slavery.

Second, to the question of whether even thinking along these lines is an insult to the saints, we should be careful not to defend the high-ground of the saints' sanctity when the saints themselves would have done no such thing. No saint would

---

[152] November 15, 1918, (12).
[153] February 10, 1919, (12).
[154] Mark 10: 43-4.

have felt inferior or jealous if he were to discover that God had given a special gift of mystical union to someone else that God had not given him. This is because the only thing that matters to saints is remaining totally receptive to whatever God might wish to give *them*.

Likewise, we too should not consider it an insult to their exalted stature to suppose that God, according to his own good will and pleasure, could have reserved a special manifestation of mystical union, even one that far surpassed their own, for a later generation.

Perhaps the attitude the saints would have expressed about the possibility of a higher holiness than their own is best captured in the concluding prayer of Cardinal Merry del Val's *Litany of Humility*: "That others may become holier than I, provided that I may become as holy as I should, Jesus, grant me the grace to desire it."

Summary: The third fiat of God and the mystery of the Incarnation

I began this evaluation of the third fiat by demonstrating how it fits within and serves the paradox of God's definitive self-Revelation. Though God in one sense completely disclosed who he is through the mystery of his Incarnation, in another sense he left his self-disclosure yet to be completed. Guided by the Spirit, man was to contemplate that mystery ever more deeply, and consequently be transformed by it ever more thoroughly, until eventually God's self-Revelation would reach Its fulfillment in and through man. Now, by the third fiat, God reveals to man the greatest depth to his already completed self-Revelation with the desire that man, in contemplating It, might be most completely transformed by It. This process would bring to completion God's first fiat of creation and his second fiat of redemption.

I close now by reviewing that same paradox through the lens of one of the most profound and elegant passages of the Second Vatican Council:

> The truth is that only in the mystery of the incarnate Word does the mystery of man take on light. For Adam, the first man, was a figure of Him Who was to come, namely Christ the Lord. Christ, the final Adam, by the revelation of the mystery of the Father and His love, fully reveals man to man himself and makes his supreme calling clear.[155]

In other words, in and through Christ's humanity: 1) God completely reveals himself to man, 2) he completely reveals man to man himself, and 3) he makes man's supreme calling completely clear. But, paradoxically, though God has made his self-Revelation entirely "complete" in each of these three respects, he has also, in each of them, left It "not yet completed" in man. In each respect, man is to gaze upon the glory of the Lord shining on the human face of Christ, and thereby be transformed from glory to glory into his very image.[156] Thus, in contemplating Christ, 1) man comes to know more completely God and his love for man, 2) man comes to know more completely who he himself is, and 3)

---

[155] *Gaudium et Spes*, 22.
[156] II Cor. 3 18, 4:6.

man comes to know more completely the nature of his supreme calling.

The third fiat of God can be most simply understood as an unexpected, new depth of insight he has given to help us most perfectly understand this tripartite pattern of his Incarnation, and most perfectly respond to It:

1) *Who is God?* God gives us a new appreciation for how he continuously radiated, and eternally radiates, his love for man within each discrete act of Christ's human existence, most especially those acts that constituted his Passion. These new insights pertain much more to what God told us through the hidden, inner acts of his human soul than they pertain to what he told us through the observable acts of his exterior life. As we now more fully appreciate God's eternal love for us as it was and is made manifest through the interior world of his humanity, we are in turn more fully transformed by and into his love.

2) *Who is man?* He helps us better understand that just as his humanity, by nature, purposefully, continuously and with infinite efficacy moved within the eternal reaches of his divinity, so can our humanity, even if only by grace. From the beginning God has created all men with the capacity to participate in the divine nature in this purposeful, continuously eternal manner. By his sin man rejected this capacity, but Jesus reclaimed it by virtue of the hypostatic union and by never separating his human willing from his divine willing. Now, by showing us more perfectly how he lived every moment of his human life "in the divine will," he shows us more perfectly who he is as a man. But by more perfectly showing us who he is as a man, he also more perfectly shows us – we who are one body with him – who we are as human beings.

3) *What is man's supreme calling?* Lastly and, among these three aspects, perhaps most singularly, he helps us better understand our supreme calling by showing us how it is bound up in our original calling to divinize the entire created order. When God created man he called man not just to co-exist with him in a static union, but to dynamically return to God all the love and glory that God had imbedded within creation. Jesus told Luisa:

> Now you ought to know that when We made Creation emerge from the Bosom of Our Divinity – because "ab eterno" it was in Us – by Us causing it to proceed from Our FIAT, We issued forth a sea of Love within which was contained all that the creature should have done. Since everything came from Us We were providers of everything it was to do. Wherefore all of Creation is replete with all the works that have to be done up to the very last man. Although it is invisible to the human eye it is visible and palpitating to Us in Our Will...[157]

By his sin, man abandoned this original calling. While it is true that God in Christ picked up that calling again and accomplished it for man, thereby fully reconciling man and the world to himself, it is also true that he wants man to repeat what he has done and thereby make it manifest.

That is, God wants man to return to his original life in the divine will and therein echo God's own eternal, creative act

---

[157] October 3, 1937, (35).

139

and his own eternal, redemptive act. Indeed, because man has not yet fully corresponded to God according to his original calling, "all creation groans and is in agony even until now."[158]

In summary, the innermost purpose of Christ's Incarnation and redemption was to return to the Father – on behalf of the creature – all the glory and love that had gone forth or ever would go forth from the Godhead into creation from the beginning of time to its end. Accomplishing this purpose was, in other words, the Son of Man's "supreme calling," and – wonder of wonders – we who are grafted into him can rightly say that it is our own supreme calling as well.

In his revelation to Luisa, Jesus offers intimate details about how he as a man responded to that call in an eternal manner by living in the divine will, and how we, in union with him, can respond to it in an eternal manner as well. As God finally sees the creature fully rise to this, his supreme, original calling, he will look upon the creature satisfied that his first fiat of creation and his second fiat of redemption have been completed. Radically hastening the coming of that day is the sum and substance of the third fiat of God.

Study and Reflection Questions

1. Review how God's works in creating and redeeming man and the universe can be considered both complete but not yet completed.

---

[158] Rom. 8:22.

2. Review how the third fiat of God can be likened to a catalyst that rapidly accelerates and brings to conclusion an already active chemical reaction.

3. If God had so willed it, would it have been possible for *someone* in the centuries after Mary and before Luisa to have lived in the divine will? If God had so willed it, would it have been possible for *no one* after Mary and before Luisa to have lived in the divine will?

4. According to St. Annibale, the divinely-appointed editor of Luisa's writings, for souls to live in the divine will they must possess heroic virtue just as the Saints of old did. What is heroic virtue? How are you striving for it in your spiritual life? He also said that for souls to live in the divine will they must first practice the "lower forms" of holiness. What are these? How are you striving to attain them?

5. What are the essential differences between Mary's fiat and Luisa's?

6. Is there any observable difference between the life of virtue and holiness that we see in the lives of the saints and the life of virtue and holiness that we see in the life of Luisa? Where, if anywhere, are any differences to be found? What does this mean for you in your own pursuit of holiness?

7. Holiness has both human and divine components that must develop together. To become more fully divine

means to become more fully human, and vice versa. How then should we understand what Jesus meant when he said that living in the divine will is a holiness that is "all divine"? Does he mean that it is any less human? What does this mean for you in your own pursuit of holiness?

IV.

CONCLUSIONS AND RECOMMENDATIONS

Orthodoxy

In the opening section, "Luisa's Obedience: the Key to her Life, Writings and Spirituality" I demonstrate that from the beginning of Luisa's extraordinary literary endeavor to its end, she wrote only out of holy obedience and with the understanding that she was to subject every word to the rightful authority of the Church. She not only accepted but welcomed the fact that there would be a secondary editorial process, and that it was to be more than a merely passive review of her writings for possible doctrinal error. The Church was to play an active, formative role to ensure that her meaning would be understood only within the boundaries of divine Revelation. In short, Luisa understood that her writings ultimately belonged not to her but to the Church, and this meant that the Church was to exercise over them an absolute interpretive authority.

Practically speaking, what does this interpretive authority presently mean? In a sense there is little need for the Church to exercise it at all, since the core theme of Luisa's literature – union with the divine will – is unambiguously orthodox. It is true that she sometimes employs what might seem to be exaggerated and problematic terminology, especially those instances which describe the "annihilation" of her human will into the divine will. But seen in context, such expressions can be fairly categorized with the "excesses of love" common to mystical literature.

It is also true that because her spirituality dwells so intently upon the divine dimension of holiness, the human dimension can be overlooked or wrongly minimized. So to forsake the human for the divine is, of course, to assume a false dichotomy, for in truth it is only by becoming more fully human that we can become more fully divine, and vice versa. But if this is a potential problem with Luisa's spirituality, it is a potential problem with any spirituality that expounds upon the divine heights of mystical union. It is not cause to reject the spirituality, but it is cause to remind the reader that, by the very mystery of the Incarnation Itself, those heights of the divine can be reached only by those determined to become more deeply anchored to the human.

The need for authoritative guidance from the Church does begin to emerge, though, as Jesus distinguishes what is novel to Luisa's experience of mystical union. "Living in the divine will" involves not only the divine will overwhelming the human will and taking over its operations, as the saints have recorded, but it also involves the creature consciously, purposefully and efficaciously participating in all of the Creator's eternal, divine activities. While Jesus repeatedly employs the qualifier, "insofar as it is possible for the creature," to make clear that these operations are only participatory, some potential for confusion remains, and a corresponding need for clarification arises. The reader should be reminded of the attributes proper to the creature, those proper only to the Creator, and those uniquely proper to Christ's human nature vis a vis the creature's.

If some form of authoritative guidance from the Church is important for properly interpreting what Luisa meant by "living in the divine will," it is acutely important for properly interpreting what she meant by "the third fiat of God." Jesus proposes that his revelation to her will, in some sense, "complete" God's first fiat of creation and his second fiat of redemption. The Church would respond by insisting that such a claim must not call into question the sufficiency of Christ's saving work and the associated sufficiency of divine Revelation.

But what is to keep the reader from reaching exactly that, and other heterodox conclusions? Despite the fact that Luisa, a faithful daughter of the Church, would not have wanted the reader to reach them, her literature in its original form fails to supply a self-evident critical framework capable of decisively preventing it from happening.

So, what sort of guidance could the Church supply? It should not and need not be a matter of bluntly superimposing a "Catholic meaning" upon them. Rather, it should only be a matter of clarifying the related Catholic teachings, and then allowing Luisa's themes to reach their own natural alignment with those teachings. For instance, the Church could clarify that since God's works of creation and redemption are already complete, anything that Luisa's revelation might "complete" about them would have to relate only to the perfection of the creature's response, and not to the perfection of the Creator's initiatives. If any passages might have been ambiguous about this point, their true meaning would emerge in light of this clarification, like iron filaments aligning themselves with the magnetic field around a bar magnet.

145

Thus, some passages would be seen more clearly to affirm that God has already done all that is necessary for the creature, while others would be seen more clearly to affirm that much yet remains to be done on the creature's part. All together these passages would clarify why God is giving this "completing" third fiat: to help the creature understand and respond to Christ's definitive Revelation "most completely." Thus, despite its lofty title and potentially problematic associated claims, Luisa's "third fiat of God" would stay within the limits of authentic private revelation.

In summary, Luisa's writings can be interpreted, and should only be interpreted, in a sense that supports and harmonizes with the principles and aims of divine Revelation as they are articulated in the teachings of the Catholic Church. I offer this book hoping to help the reader interpret her writings in just such a way, that is, not only to avoid possible confusion and misunderstanding but also to give her spirituality the final shape it needs to fully achieve its intended purposes. Though the views I offer here are only my own and do not amount to "authoritative guidance," I offer them only after having made every effort to make them consonant with the Magisterium of the Church.

Finally, I offer this book in anticipation of, and in complete deference to, all forms of authoritative guidance that may subsequently come from the Church, most especially from the Holy See and the Archdiocese of Trani – Barletta – Bisceglie and Titular of Nazareth (the Archdiocese responsible for Luisa's cause).

Edifying Value

So long as Luisa's writings are read as she intended them to be read, that is, planted within the rich soil of Catholic Tradition and thereinafter nurtured, new fields of spiritual fruit can issue forth from them. Saint Annibale di Francia says it well in his General Preface to her writings:

> In many ways these revelations open new horizons, not yet contemplated until now, concerning the mysteries of the Divine Will, and about operating and living in It. And one thing is certain: even before arriving at the complete knowledge of what it means to operate and live in the Divine Volition, one who reads these writings cannot *not* remain enamored with the Will of God, and *not* feel new strong impulses, and a divine commitment to transforming all of himself in the Divine Will.

Anyone familiar with the transforming union – as St. Annibale certainly was – understands how stunning are his words, "not yet contemplated until now." And yet that is the sense that emerges from a study of her spirituality. God lifts the creature into the eternal horizons of his own divine life, wherein the creature might again see, enjoy and employ all the splendors of his original unity with the divine will. Luisa's spirituality, corresponding to the traditional Christian framework of prayer, opens these new horizons into a life in the divine will in two ways.

First, her spirituality offers a system of practices that help order the human will toward a state of habitual unity within the divine will. The same ways of radical detachment, penance and asceticism that have always been foundational to the spiritual life remain so here, re-affirmed and encouraged as much by the witness of Luisa's life as by her writings. What she uniquely offers, though, is a new pattern of discursive prayer (or meditation) especially intended to aid the creature in habitually ascending to the eternal mode of participation in the divine life.

Known as the "rounds" of creation and redemption, these prayers take up the traditional themes of meditative prayer – such as union with the sufferings of Christ, delight in God's love for man and in his handiwork in creation, and so forth – and lift them to a new, eternal horizon. Like all discursive prayer, the conceptual structures of the rounds eventually give way to the simple, non-conceptual experience of contemplation. But the core desires expressed by those structures persist, and in fact they are intensified as the soul moves beyond the conceptual dimension of living in the divine will and into its contemplative dimension.

It is there, in contemplation, that Luisa's writings open new horizons in a second way. In many respects, what she tells us about living in the divine will only repeats a pattern well known to the Catholic spiritual tradition. After the soul has been prepared by the conceptual structures of discursive prayer and by a variety of other human efforts aided by grace, the Lord then suspends the operations of the intellect and lifts the soul into a non-conceptual loving awareness of God. God effectively absorbs what is human into the field of his own divine operations. The human manner of prayer gives way to the divine manner. But however imponderable and exalted our previous experiences of this state might have been, Luisa's account shows us how God could yet open from within this state a new and deeper horizon.

Now not only does God fully take over all of our actions, but he also invites and empowers us to fully share in all of his own creative and redemptive actions, even as they reach to and include every corner and moment of created existence. In the most elevated sense, we lay claim to our identity in Christ: we have become *everything* that God is, apart from the identity of substance.

Moreover, we become aware that this state of maximal union with God is charged with purpose. With and in Christ, we pick up where our first parents left off by lifting all of creation – in the past, the present and the future – to the glory of the Father. Thus, Luisa shows us "living in the divine will" as man's consummate response of gratitude, praise and reparation to God, indeed a response in which the ultimate destiny of creation is bound up.

Will everyone who accepts God's invitation so to live in his divine will perceive that experience as clearly and profoundly as Luisa did? Certainly not, but what matter is that? As with any mystic's experience, if the Lord has allowed Luisa to see this experience of intimate union with him with special clarity, it is only for the sake of those of us not graced to see it as clearly. "God calls us all to this intimate union with him, even if the special graces or extraordinary signs of this mystical life are granted only to some for the sake of manifesting the gratuitous gift given to all."[159]

---

[159] CCC #2014.

So, whether it is perceived in contemplation only as an inkling or in all of its stunning splendor, God bestows the same fundamental reality of living in the divine will upon anyone who sincerely desires it.

Plausibility

Even if it is possible – and I believe it is – to view Luisa's spirituality within an orthodox framework, and even if within this framework her spirituality can offer edifying value – and I believe it can – the associated claims can still stagger the mind. Is it really possible that God would have waited two thousand years to show man the consummate mode of responding to him? That he would have bound up in that response the very fulfillment of his works of creation and redemption? Moreover, that he would show man that response through a private revelation to a simple, bed-ridden woman in southern Italy? And even if we can answer, yes, in theory all of this is possible, we might yet ask: Is it *likely* that God would act in such a way?

I close this study by offering a few thoughts, admittedly more intuitive than analytical, about why I lean toward answering, yes, to that final question as well.

First, while to claim that God is only now, two thousand years after the fact, disclosing the core purpose of the redemption, does tend to shock and outrage, God does like to surprise us. Of course, his ways are always constant, but they are also always unpredictable. He is ever ancient, ever new. Before Jesus ascended to heaven, he promised he would ultimately complete his work in and through us, but he left us to wonder exactly how he would do it. Since then, we have known only that he would complete his work in us in a manner continuous with his definitive self-Revelation. So, the fact that this consummating third fiat of God comes to us in the form of a radical "surprise in continuity" seems to be more of a reason to accept it than not.

Second, Luisa's revelations are written down in a form that would seem to authenticate their divine origin. Judged as a body of literature, her writings do not rise to the level of the spiritual classics. On the contrary, a number of stumbling blocks confront the reader: her syntax and grammar are often clumsy, her meaning vague, her style tedious. She had neither the talent of a writer nor the desire to be one, and it clearly shows. But somehow, through the fumbling pen of this minimally educated, culturally isolated woman, shines a sublimity that is, to my reckoning, unparalleled in the annals of mystical literature. The messages she conveys would certainly seem to be divine in origin, but perhaps in anticipation of readers who might wish to ascribe a merely human origin to them, Jesus delivered them through a human vessel who, without doubt, would have been among the least capable of originating them.

Third, the likelihood that all this is of God is supported by the very fact of Luisa's enduring obscurity. Even after thousands of pages of diary entries, spread out over some forty years, what we see of this little woman herself is barely an outline. What we do see are the glory of God shining through the heretofore hidden, innermost depths of Christ's humanity, and Luisa, a tiny speck of a human person, lost within that mystery. A hidden woman to begin with, we see that throughout her extraordinary spiritual journey she perpetually refuses to draw any attention to herself. On the contrary, as Jesus lifts her into this role of singular significance, she disappears into him all the more thoroughly. She thereby not only authenticates her revelation, she models her spirituality.

A fourth indicator that this surprising, new plan for man is likely to be of God is the thematic elegance with which it comprehensively and uniquely interconnects man's origin with his destiny. For the creature to fully, consciously reclaim, in this life, all the dignities he abandoned and forgot at the fall, in order that he might finally divinize all of creation for the Father, does indeed seem to represent the consummation of Christ's recapitulation. It does make more sense than not that the ultimate destiny of creation would be bound up in man's consummate response to God, and that the form of that response would somehow be linked to man's origins. But if that is so, it is fair to ask: Who else, in the preceding twenty centuries, has so thoroughly restated, much less reclaimed, those ultimate, transcendent purposes that were imbedded within the state of man's original unity with God?

A fifth indicator of a divine origin to this grand plan for man is the fact that the sole means of accomplishing it is by shedding new light upon the mystery of the Incarnation, and, by implication, the mystery of the human person. In the end, the "third fiat of God" emerges as nothing more and nothing less than God holding up a mirror to man's face, or, more precisely, God opening up a new dimension within the mirror that he has already held up to man. Thus, if living in the divine will can be called a "new" gift to man, it is not as something alien foisted upon him from without, but as something ineffably familiar drawn forth from within. What is that ineffable familiarity?

In a word, eternity. Created in the image of the One who is Eternity Itself, man has from the dawn of creation moved through his earthly life perpetually yearning, whether consciously or not, for the eternal. Heaven alone can ultimately satisfy that deepest longing, but man yet yearns to satisfy it in this life as well.

In this sense, it could be said that man has yearned for thousands of years to hear what Jesus tells Luisa: how while yet on earth man might do the will of the Father eternally, that is, as the blessed do his will in heaven. Jesus shows us how, simply by opening up before us the eternal, divine horizons compenetrated by his own humanity. Thus, seeing more clearly the inner mystery of who he is, we see more clearly the inner mystery of who we were created to be, and, in him, the inner mystery of who we in fact already are.

Appendix

November 1, 2012 letter from
Archbishop Giovanni Pichierri

Prot. N. 182/12/C3

COMMUNICATION n°. 3
About the process of Beatification and Canonization
of the Servant of God *LUISA PICCARRETA*

Addressing the many who, in different ways in the world, are interested in the Servant of God *Luisa Piccarreta* and the spirituality of *Living in the Divine Will*, I like to update what I have previously reported on several occasions, and above all in the *Communications* of April 23, 2007 and of May 30, 2008.

The diffusion in the world of the figure and writings of the Servant of God Luisa Piccarreta has grown considerably in recent years, reaching new nations in all continents. Letters from Bishops, priests, and lay persons alike give proof of this, as well as the record of visitors to the places related to Luisa in Corato.

The joy of witnessing the growth of this reality is accompanied by the concern to extend to all a heartfelt **appeal for unity** and the mutual esteem, rejecting "quarreling and jealousy" as one who waits for the advent of the "fullness of day" (Rm 13:11-14). If we live in the light of the Divine Will we cannot but cultivate in ourselves the fruits of mutual Charity, for "anyone who claims to be in the light but hates his brother is still in the darkness, " (1 Jn 2:9).

I still observe with sorrow that "the doctrine of the Divine Will has not always been presented in a correct and respectful way, according to the doctrine and the Magisterium of the Church, putting remarks in the mouth of Luisa that are not even implicitly found in her writings. This provokes a trauma in consciences and even confusion and rejection among the people and by some Priests and Bishops" (*Letter* of March 9, 2006).

Therefore, it is my duty to point out some directions in a way that is clear for all.

Current state of the Cause

1. Actor of the process of Beatification and Canonization is the "*Association "Luisa Piccarreta - Little Children of the Divine Will"* of Corato, that with its new statute dated June 13, 2010, I wanted to constitute as a Public Association of the Faithfu due to its particular ecclesial significance.

2. I have given the Association a mandate in 2006 to constitute the *Secretariat of the Cause of Beatification of the Servant of God Luisa Piccarreta*, as an organism of liaison, support and information at the service of the many who in various ways are interested in the Cause itself, with the further task of opening dialogue with other Dioceses, persons, groups, and associations. "The Archdiocese and the Association will use *exclusively* the Secretariat to receive and answer any request made to them" (*Communication* of April 23, 2007). Therefore, no person or Association in the world can issue official notice apart from this Secretariat. *I forbid anyone from attempting to do so in my name.*

3. In 1994, with the *non obstare* of the Holy See was opened the Diocesan Inquiry into the life, virtues and fame of sanctity. This was concluded on October 29, 2005 with the transmission of

1

the Proceedings to the Congregation for the Causes of Saints and the nomination of Dr. Silvia Monica Correale as Postulator and Rev. Fr. Sabino Amedeo Lattanzio as Vice-postulator. The Congregation subsequently has communicated to me that "before proceeding *any further*, an examination of the writings of the Servant of God will be done, in order to clarify difficulties of a theological nature."

4. In the prayerful anticipation of the outcome of this examination, I wish to address *all those who claim that these writings contain doctrinal errors*. This, to date, has never been endorsed by any pronouncement by the Holy See, nor personally by myself. I would like to note that in this way, in addition to anticipate the legitimate judgment of the Church, these persons cause scandal to the faithful who are spiritually nourished by said writings, originating also suspicion of those of us who are zealous in the pursuit of the Cause. In the anticipation of the judgment by competent Authority, I invite you to make more serious and in-depth meditations and reflections in your personal reading on these writings in light of Sacred Scripture, Tradition, and the Magisterium of the Church.

5. Furthermore, I wish to reiterate that if the writings of the Servant of God are read by people as to lead to the formation of one or more groups, this should not occur against the will of the Ordinary of the Place. Likewise, I recall what I have already communicated: "Neither the Archdiocese nor the Association nor the Secretariat has delegated any person, group or other association, in any way, to represent them outside of their legitimate locations, to spread knowledge about the life, thought and writings of the Servant of God or to make any decision in their names. From the moment that the Diocesan Inquiry was begun, the Archdiocese has never officially designated any Theologian or Censor for the writing of Luisa. Likewise, it has never nominated any official translator of the writings from Italian into any other language" (*Communication* of April 23, 2007).

Preparation of the *typical edition* of the writings

6. "As I have already expressed at the conclusion of the diocesan phase of the Cause, it is my desire, after having heard the opinion of the Congregation for the Causes of Saints, to present *a typical and critical edition of the writings* in order to provide the faithful with a trustworthy text of the writings of Luisa Piccarreta. So I repeat, the said writings are *exclusively the property of the Archdiocese*" (Letter to Bishops of October 14, 2006). To accomplish this demanding work that requires a certain kind of competence, I shall avail myself of a team of experts chosen in agreement with the Postulation.

7. Nevertheless, I must mention the growing and unchecked flood of transcriptions, translations and publications both through print and the internet. At any rate, "seeing the delicacy of the current phase of the proceedings, any and every publication of the writings is *absolutely* forbidden at this time. Anyone who acts against this is disobedient and greatly harms the cause of the Servant of God. " (*Communication* of May 30, 2008). All effort must be invested in avoiding all "leaks" of publications of any kind.

Groups of the Divine Will

8. "It is with great joy that I receive the news that more and more of the groups that are inspired by the Divine Will are strengthening their community links with their diocesan Bishops, so creating that indispensable communion within the local Church and so allowing any possible tension or division to be overcome" (*Communication* of May 30, 2008). I reiterate, therefore, that "initiatives that are taken in reference with the spirituality of Luisa, for example conferences, spiritual retreats, prayer meetings, etc., must be authorized by one's Bishop in

2

157

order to give serenity to the participants" (Letter of November 24, 2003).

9. Necessary prudence cannot lessen the ardor of those who feel compelled to spread the knowledge of the sanctity of life of the Servant of God, or of those who recommend the reading of her writings, or of those who encourage the faithful prayer for her beatification. All this not only is not prohibited, rather very much desirable. I also invite you to "reinforce the unity and communion among the dioceses in which individuals, groups and associations inspired by the Servant of God Luisa Piccarreta, and who know her writings, are to be found" (Final Communication of October 28, 2005).

What is asked of those familiar with Luisa Piccarreta

1. To pray for the Beatification of the Servant of God, that the Most Holy Trinity might be glorified and be diffuse the Reign of the Divine Will.
2. To send to the Postulation, through the Secretariat the testimonies and all else that regards the Servant of God, together with the economic donations needed today more than ever, for the work of the *"typical edition"* of the writings of Luisa.
3. To create a network of links between the several groups united with their Bishop, and our own Archdiocese, to make visible, ever more the great family of the *Divine Will*, established in the bond of unity, of the ecclesial communion and of the commitment of the new evangelization for the tradition of faith.

With great friendship and warmth, I greet and bless you all.

Trani, November 1st, 2012

✠ *Giovan Battista Pichierri*
Archbishop

3

158

www.ingramcontent.com/pod-product-compliance
Lightning Source LLC
Chambersburg PA
CBHW051837090426
42736CB00011B/1848